D1208620

THIS HAPPENED IN PASADENA

THE MACMILLAN COMPANY
NEW YORK • BOSTON • CHICAGO
DALLAS • ATLANTA • SAN FRANCISCO

MACMILLAN AND CO., LIMITED
LONDON • BOMBAY • CALCUTTA
MADRAS • MELBOURNE

THE MACMILLAN COMPANY
OF CANADA, LIMITED
TORONTO

THIS HAPPENED IN PASADENA

by David Hulburd

The Macmillan Company: New York

1951

PRINTED IN THE UNITED STATES OF AMERICA

First Printing

To Meg and Roger Egeberg
with much affection

I am deeply grateful to the many people in Pasadena who were so generous with their time and help when I was gathering material for this book.

David Hulburd
San Francisco,
March, 1951

Introduction

We believe this to be a singular book—one that we feel not only privileged to publish but also obligated to publish, in the sense that certain kinds of books deserve to be undertaken as a form of public service.

We deliberately use that sometimes misused phrase because we believe that a book dealing with public education performs in a very real way a service to the public. For education, like freedom, is everybody's job.

The kind of education our children are getting now will to a large extent determine the kind of citizens they will become. This has always been a truism; but today, with an estimated increase over normal years of more than a million children about to enter school in the near future—making the largest elementary school enrollment in the history of the country—it is a more important consideration than ever.

The fact that not enough widespread interest and attention has been given to the matter of public education lends even more cogency to the publication of a book that poses specific and pertinent questions, problems, and issues regarding the status of our school systems.

Every teacher, every school administrator, every parent, taxpayer, and voter has a vital stake in the future of public education in the United States. The management of a school system is the immediate responsibility of local Boards of Education the country over, but the ultimate responsibility for the shaping and development of that system rests with the electorate; it is up to the voters to decide on the composition of their Boards.

But do voters, in general, recognize their prerogatives and their responsibilities? Do they, in fact, go to the polls and vote for their Board members? Do they know what kind of education they want their children to receive and do they take the trouble to find out by what means teachers and administrators provide it? Do they inquire how they can work, as a community, with their schools for the common educational good? And do they understand that the independence of the American public-school system constitutes its greatest strength, and that the perpetuation of freedom in the United States depends in large part upon the quality of public education that they are able to maintain? These are salient questions.

It is our hope that this book, written by a journalist, not an educator, will reach a broad audience; that it will be read and discussed not only by those in the field of education, whose interest in it will be professional, but also by those not directly connected with educational activities. It is our aim and, again, our hope that this book will stimulate serious thought regarding the questions noted above—all of which were dramatically raised and high-lighted by "the Pasadena affair."

In 1948, the Pasadena Board of Education, anxious to meet the demands of an exacting future with a forward-looking school administration, carefully selected as its new Superintendent of Schools a man who, in the opinion of his colleagues, represented praiseworthy and desirable educational ideals and standards. Willard Goslin, at the time of his appointment by the Pasadena Board, was president of the American Association of

School Administrators, the highest honor that can be bestowed on a public educator in this country. He accepted his new post at Pasadena willingly and he was gratefully received.

Two and a half years later, however, the same Board that hired him requested his resignation. And thereby hangs a tale which is of national significance. This book tells that story, fully and factually.

Mr. Goslin was the focal point of the controversy that blazed in Pasadena in the fall of 1950. But this is not the story of a personal martyrdom. It is what Willard Goslin stood for and fought against that deserves our attention. An analysis of what happened in Pasadena provides a lesson of grave importance: any school system in the country is alarmingly vulnerable today to attack from outside the local community as well as from within.

It is a fact that certain forces, vicious, well organized, and coldly calculating, would like to change the face of education in the United States. This they must not be allowed to do. Well meaning and honest citizens must recognize these forces and refuse to be used to further their ends. At the same time local pressure groups, quite unaware of influences operating outside the community, must themselves be carefully scrutinized with regard to their motives, their tactics, and the "reforms" they would effect. The members of such groups are in need of self-appraisal. Are they acting for the ultimate civic good or for a shortsighted and selfish personal end?

In Pasadena the school system was simultaneously a victim of both ailments, in that it fell prey to pressures within the city limits and to infiltrating influences originating thousands of miles away. Both had a direct bearing on the eventual ousting of Mr. Goslin and his liberal school administration. If that outcome was a victory for the few, it was a severe shock to many an average Pasadenan.

This first full blow-by-blow account of the issues, personalities, and sequence of events involved in the Pasadena school controversy touches upon a great many of the sources of country-wide friction over public-school affairs. The record given here should be of profound concern to every American, for what happened in Pasadena, a community favored above the average for the encouragement of a sound and beneficent school system, can happen in towns and cities throughout all our forty-eight states.

It must be remembered that no community deserves a better school system than it is willing to pay for, work for, and care about.

—THE PUBLISHERS

1

Mr. Goslin Goes to Atlantic City

In Minneapolis, one cold February night of 1948, a man named Goslin, who was superintendent of the city's public schools, boarded an airliner and headed East. Under any ordinary set of circumstances Willard Goslin would have been a pleased and happy man. As a person of consequence in the very professional world of education, Mr. Goslin was on his way to Atlantic City, where, the next day, he was to be installed as president of the American Association of School Administrators, the highest honor the highest administrative body in public education in the United States can bestow. In Atlantic City also, he had a date to meet four members of the City of Pasadena, three men and a woman who had traveled three thousand miles from their pleasant and proud little city to find a new superintendent for their schools.

That was all very well, but Mr. Goslin was leaving Minneapolis under anything but an ordinary set of circumstances. At the moment every last school building was shut tight because the teachers' union had called a strike, and some 65,000 school children were celebrating an unfortunate winter's holiday. The school system itself was a worn-out piece of machinery. As superintendent, Mr. Goslin stood squarely in the middle of an impossible situation: an antiquated charter, an outmoded tax-collection procedure, insufficient levies, an almost empty till, and a budget-balancing system that seemed to have as one of its main precepts the reduction of teachers' salaries. All the attempts of certain civic-minded industrialists to bring about a solution had had little effect on a rather apathetic citizenry and a school Board split wide open by dissension. Willard Goslin was now left with no place to turn, after two years of futile negotiation. And he was a tired man.

Not that Willard Goslin wasn't used to tough times. During his twenty-three years in education, most of them as a superintendent of schools, he had had at least his share, and possibly more than his share, of hard knocks. But he was willing to take it, so long as he felt he was doing some good for the community and for education. He had been taking it for a long time.

Willard Goslin was born and raised on a worn-out farm in middle Missouri, a lean, lanky fellow who hunted possum, trapped muskrat, milked cows, walked two miles to school (sometimes barefoot), and thinned corn at 75 cents a day for spending money. He began teaching school at sixteen. He worked his way through college, was made a high-school principal when he was only twenty-two, and the superintendent of a small system in Slater, Missouri, when he was twenty-three. From that job he was fired because he was thought too blamed aggressive by the town's more staid, not to say moss-backed, residents. In 1928 he was appointed superintendent of schools at Webster Groves, an upper-middle-class, moderately rich suburb of St. Louis with, then, a population of 18,000. On his first day in office, Mr. Goslin shifted an oldster out of his job as principal of one of the schools and into what some thought was a sinecure, at slightly higher pay—a move Mr. Goslin was convinced was sound procedure. That brought down on his head a flock of angry protests from citizens who loved the old fellow and thought he should keep his principalship, come hell, high water, or Willard Goslin. Mr. Goslin stood his ground, soothed tempers, kept peace with his school Board, and stayed on at Webster Groves for fifteen happy years. Then he went on to Minneapolis.

Now, as Mr. Goslin flew toward his Eastern appointments this February night, he was not sure what he wanted to do, or what his next step would be—if, indeed, it would be anything other than staying on in Minneapolis. He knew little about the Pasadena post or, for that matter, about Pasadena itself. Only the November before, the president of the Pasadena Board of Education had written him a letter, misspelling Goslin, asking if he would be good enough to suggest the names "of three persons whom [*sic*] you think are qualified for the position of superintendent"—a position to be open the following July. The Board president did not invite Mr. Goslin to submit his own name, and, in his reply, written the last day of the year, Mr. Goslin politely did not do so. It was, then, something of a surprise for him to get a letter only seven days later, this time signed by the secretary of Pasadena's Board, asking if he would meet its members in Atlantic City as a possible candidate himself for superintendent of their schools.

Mr. Goslin's reply could be considered typical of his direct and forthright approach to any problem: He would be "glad to visit with" the Board in Atlantic City, but gave them to understand that he was not seeking the job. "However, if your Board of Education is genuinely interested in my possibilities or the development of an understanding of my possibilities as superintendent of schools of your city, then it seems that it might be well for someone to brief me on the steps which you are taking in an attempt to select a superintendent of schools."

"I would," he continued, "evaluate a position first in terms of the freedom which it accords for educational leadership at local, state, and national levels; then I would be interested in the opportunities to maintain and develop a superior professional staff at all levels of the school systems; and finally I would need to give attention to the matter of salary and related items." Thus, on January 26, 1948, before he had set eyes on the school Board, before he had seen the modern city of Pasadena, before he had been more than mentioned in passing as a possibility for the post, Mr. Goslin unequivocally laid it on the line. He never had been, was not then, and never was to be the kind of man who washed his educational theories and desires with soft soap.

It was snowing when Mr. Goslin reached Atlantic City the following morning after his flight from Minneapolis. After breakfast, he went to his eleven o'clock meeting with the Pasadena Board of Education. The four members received him cordially in a bedroom in the Dennis Hotel. On hand were the Board's president, a portly gentleman named Vernon Brydolf; William L. Blair, twenty years on the Board, a man straight-standing as a ramrod and with hair white as the snow outside; Milton Wopschall, then but thirty years old and with only one year's Board service behind him; and Miss Harriet Sterling, a maiden lady who, like Mr. Wopschall, was a freshman member. Fifth and only other member of the Board, Mrs. Gladys Rinehart, had not been able to come East because of illness in her family.

In his deep, resonant voice, Vernon Brydolf expressed his pleasure at meeting Mr. Goslin, about whom they'd all heard so much; and then, for ten hardly momentous minutes, he proceeded to tell Mr. Goslin something about Pasadena's three school districts: their history, their status, the problems of their budgets, and their plans. No controversial issues were brought up, and no direct reference was made to so-called Progressive, or Modern, Education. Then, to the mild surprise of the Board members, and possibly to the flattery of some, Mr. Goslin proceeded to ask each one of them a few questions. Mr. Brydolf said that he was an attorney-at-law in Pasadena. Mr. Wopschall was in a wholesale paint business founded by his father. Miss Sterling had taught school for thirty-five years, most of them in Pasadena, and was now retired. Mr. Blair was the associate editor of the *Star-News*, one of the two local newspapers, and wrote a daily column for it. Mrs. Rinehart, they told him, was a housewife, a mother, and an old hand at Parent-Teacher Association affairs. Truly, this was a crosscut of the community, typical of Boards of Education the nation over. And as talk went on, they gave Mr. Goslin every assurance, without precisely saying so, that, from what they knew of his educational theories and practices, his were not essentially different from those of the man he would succeed: John A. Sexson, who was retiring the following June after two decades on the job, and who, Mr. Goslin didn't need to be told, had laid the foundation of Modern Education in Pasadena.

In his turn, Mr. Goslin briefly outlined for them his educational philosophy—a subject on which he was always glad to expound—especially as it pertained to the community. He was convinced that the community was the central core of education, with the superintendent, as educational leader, assuming a prominent role and not simply operating as an administrator. No one offered any objection to this view. Miss Sterling and Mr. Wopschall, the two newest members, contributed their own belief that they felt a need for a superintendent who was sympathetic to the teaching staff; and, indeed, this was a most natural desire, but later, much later, Mr. Goslin was to have cause for contemplating most earnestly various interpretations of what they said.

Before the pleasant little gathering had broken up, the Board members implied that they were interested in Mr. Goslin for the job; and he, returning the compliment but without committing himself, let it be known that he might entertain an offer. Naturally, it was agreed that it would be wise for him to have a firsthand look at Pasadena, and at Pasadena's school system. Matters rested there for the moment. Mr. Goslin bade them all a friendly goodbye and went on to meet his convention schedule. Later that day he was duly installed as president of the American Association of School Administrators, and was soon on his way back to Minneapolis.

When he got there, Mr. Goslin found that no progress had been made toward settling the teachers' strike. And for twenty-four more days the deadlock continued through a hopeless and almost endless series of meetings, negotiations, propositions, and counterpropositions. When it finally ended and the score had been tallied, it was generally agreed that the teachers had won a small victory—a victory which could have been won, for all the good it did anyone, the very first day. It was generally agreed that Willard Goslin had emerged unscathed, except in his own deep feeling that, because he had been the central figure in this local tragedy of civic neglect, his usefulness as a superintendent had been impaired.

The strike ended on March 23. Meanwhile a cordial invitation had come to him from the Pasadena Board of Education: Would he visit Pasadena for a day or so, and see how he liked the city and its school system? The California Education Code specifically forbidding the importation of outlanders on expense accounts, Mr. Goslin would be brought in, according to established and honorable custom, as a consultant, at $100 a day. Mr. Goslin accepted with pleasure, and on March 25 advised the Board's president that he would arrive on March 31. "I just want to be turned loose in the community," he wrote, "to see if I can get a feeling of the situation, both in and out of the school system. . . ."

2

The City on the Arroyo

One way for the busy tourist to have a quick look at Pasadena is to get on its most famous street and stay on it through all its perambulations. This he may do by driving twelve miles out the Arroyo Seco Freeway from Los Angeles and, when he comes to a sign reading Orange Grove Avenue, leaving the Freeway, driving up to the overpass, taking a sharp left, and then just going on.

Orange Grove Avenue rises, like a mountain-fed stream, in South Pasadena. Soon it flows west and becomes South Orange Grove Avenue, and by then the tourist is in Pasadena proper. The street is wide and is lined with tall and handsome palm trees. Most of the rich and respectable citizens of Pasadena once lived on South Orange Grove Avenue, and some of them still do, in huge old blocks that remind an Easterner of Palm Beach. Some of the houses are now beginning to show signs of decay; here and there one of them, possibly to save taxes, has been torn down and not replaced, leaving gaps that give the street the look of an aging and once handsome dowager who has lost a few front teeth. The old Busch place, a thirty-acre garden spot built from a beer fortune, has now been cut up for a super-residential section, but the Wrigley place is still a monument to gum, and South Orange Grove remains a stately landmark of a nearly bygone era.

As soon as he has crossed Colorado Street, at a point just a few blocks from where Colorado becomes the city's principal business thoroughfare, the tourist is on North Orange Grove. Then he drops down a hill, passes a few unidentifiable and smaller estates, and soon comes upon a sign directing him to the Rose Bowl. From this point the street begins to deteriorate. Now there are shingle and frame houses which, as he proceeds, become even less opulent in appearance. By this time he has made nearly a complete semicircle almost without knowing it, and is on East Orange Grove. Soon he crosses Fair Oaks, the boundary of the nonwhite settlement, the street containing many of the city's small industries. Even this small segment of the Negro and Mexican district which the tourist sees is, comparatively speaking, hardly substandard. It could never be called a slum.

Before long, East Orange Grove widens out, and the tourist begins to see again what he often sees in Pasadena—one-story houses finished in stucco or shingle, each with its tiny lawn, each with its own private view of the sun.

Now, as the traveler drives east, the street broadens into a six-lane boulevard, and its fine small residences, although not in a class with the piles on South Orange Grove, indicate substance and solidity. It is in houses like these that a great many Pasadenans live, and wait for their particular suns to set.

There is much to Pasadena that is not a part of its necklace of orange groves. Many wealthier families live in the Oak Knoll district, with its majestic old live oaks flanking the streets, its Huntington Hotel as a social center, and its many mausoleum-like dwellings. East Pasadena is fashionable too, along such streets as Lombardy, where the architecture runs to Colonial, Old English, and Spanish. Other residents, however, prefer living in the hills on the other side of the Arroyo Seco—which means dry river—across Colorado Street's famous bridge. And in these hills, off Linda Vista and San Rafael, the homeowner can get the best view of the city itself, and of Mount Wilson rising behind it.

The interested tourist, having satisfied his geographical curiosity, could discover other facts about Pasadena: It has its own suburb in the foothills to the north—Altadena, which is part of the same school district. It has one of the most modern, best laid-out department stores in the United States—Bullock's Pasadena, owned by an enterprising family of Los Angeles merchants. Colorado Street is unique in that it is the only consequential thoroughfare of mercantile establishments in the whole of this city of more than 100,000 inhabitants. The Pasadena Playhouse in its thirty years has put on some 1,500 plays on its three stages, and is known far and wide as a training ground for actors. The single main track of the Santa Fe runs at street level through the heart of the city, carrying with painful caution its Chief and Super Chief at ten miles per hour. On New Year's morning the Tournament of Roses, sponsored by downtown merchants for sound commercial motives as well as for reasons of civic pride, entertains untold thousands of spectators annually with a seemingly never ending series of floats. That same afternoon the Rose Bowl, owned by the city, is host to the most widely publicized football game in the world. Pasadena's two newspapers, the middle-of-the-road *Star-News* and the sometimes sensational *Independent,* feed the citizens an interesting compound of local, national, and international news. And right next door to Pasadena, in San Marino, the justly renowned Huntington Library is a lasting memorial to a great Californian.

Possibly the most surprising thing about Pasadena is that it is, actually, in every sense of the word, a city. True, each morning a vast horde of businessmen climb into their well polished automobiles, turn briskly down into the Freeway, and are soon in the heart of Los Angeles, just like commuters in Greenwich, Connecticut, or Lake Forest, Illinois, or Burlingame, California. But whereas Greenwich and Lake Forest and Burlingame and a host of similar towns are primarily suburbs of the cities they feed, Pasadena, even though it is so suffocatingly close to Los Angeles, enjoys a great measure of self-sufficiency. It is not, the way Glendale once was, merely a bedroom of Los Angeles. Many of its citizens never go near Los Angeles, and think of Hollywood as a never-never land thousands of miles away.

During the past ten years, a number of small industries were established within the city's limits, and the population rose from 81,000 to 104,000—a fact which in itself was to pose its special problems. An accurate estimate of the worth of these industries has never been reckoned, but they include a wide variety of manufactured goods such as precision instruments, gifts, chemicals, foods, pharmaceuticals, optical supplies, shoes, fine printing, and scientific instruments. And although it is not a small business, but a large and flourishing cultural enterprise, the California Institute of Technology, with an annual budget of $8,000,000, and some 2,000 people on its payroll, is a home-grown project of which all Pasadena is understandably proud.

Among the many figures available on Pasadena's national

standing, some are significant and pertinent. In 1949 *Sales Management* magazine reported that the city's per capita net effective buying power—that is, what each citizen could spend if he wanted to—was fifth highest in the country, a total of $249,745,000 that year for its 39,000 families; and that was an increase of almost $15,000,000 over the year before. Although it ranks 104th in population, it ranks fifty-second in furniture, house, and radio sales. A recent housing survey indicated that 71 per cent of the residences in Pasadena are owned by the families living in them—a fact that looms uncomfortably large whenever it comes time to try to raise real-estate taxes. Even its substandard housing would hardly alarm a social worker: its density of population is 17.2 persons per acre as against 7.49 for the city as a whole and, again, against a density per acre of 272 in one of Los Angeles's most crowded areas.

As for the growth of the colored population, recent figures are not available, but it is interesting to note that whereas in 1920 the colored population of the city was 1,094, or 2 per cent of the city's total of 45,000, by 1946 it had risen to 6,326, which meant a little over 6 per cent of the 98,000 persons then in Pasadena. Any such growth of lower-income and nonwhite groups, even though not large, is never greeted happily by those who are interested in maintaining residential property values; and in a place like Pasadena, where tradition and conformity play such a large role, this unhappiness is most apparent. But the fact remains that, in this city which has graduated from being merely an attraction for tourists and retired oldsters and rich winter visitors to a point where it is now a thriving industrial community, such growth is normal and healthy. There has never been a race riot in Pasadena. Its

Negroes and its Mexicans, like its whites, live in dignity, privacy, and peace.

This, then, was the city Willard Goslin prepared to visit in March of 1948—a city of culture and salubrious climate (when the newfangled smog hadn't closed in), a city of better than average means where a number of its retired citizens live on annuities, a city blessed with unusual advantages for the cultivation and encouragement of a fine school system, and, above all, a city which, with its new working population, was beginning to show signs, beneath its placid exterior, of restless social change and of an acceptance of a changing world. Perhaps, before long, no one would be able to say, as a whimsical visitor once observed, that Pasadena has its own set of the three R's: Rich, Reactionary, and Republican.

3

A Visit, an Offer, and a Decision

Mr. Goslin put in two exceedingly busy hundred-dollar days in Pasadena. He met many men of consequence, visited with the ladies of the Board and their friends, lunched with the League of Women Voters and others, took notes and made mental observations on what he saw. One day a car and driver were put at his disposal and he spent the afternoon prowling the city. One night he walked, alone, from one end of the business section of Colorado Street to the other. He courteously paid a call on the retiring superintendent, John Sexson, a shrewd and sage oldster who had known an earlier day when the going was rough in Pasadena for a Progressive-minded school man. With more than a little pleasure, Mr. Goslin met a friend he had known back in Missouri, now Pasadena's deputy superintendent of schools. "I had a quality of favorable reaction toward George Merideth when I saw him again in Pasadena," Mr. Goslin said later, "and I felt comfortable about him. I was glad to know he'd be there if I took the job."

By the time Mr. Goslin settled down to a long lunch with the entire school Board, there seemed to be a tacit understanding around the table that the superintendency was his if he wanted it. For a time, indeed, conversation centered around the fact that, should he come to Pasadena, Mr. Goslin must, inevitably, spend a great deal of time on the road as president of the School Administrators. Mr. Goslin warned the Board members of that. The Board members understood and approved.

On his way back to Minneapolis, Mr. Goslin stopped off in the Pacific Northwest for a few speaking engagements and a few days' vacation. There he had time to reflect on his visit to Pasadena. What he had seen, he liked. Long ago he had made up his mind he would never again be superintendent of schools in a privileged suburban community like Webster Groves. For a time he had been afraid Pasadena would be like it. But to his surprise and pleasure he had found elements there that were attractive to his active and imaginative mind. For one thing, its school system, while by no means perfect—"I wouldn't have been interested if it *had* been perfect"—was certainly on the right track. The fundamentals were there, ranging from such mundane considerations as a fine set of IBM machinery for the business department to such recondite matters as a preschool child-training program and, as he termed it, "some pieces of a good modern educational curriculum." Not the least important of these, established in Pasadena by John Sexson some years back—the first of its kind in the country—was the so-called 6-4-4 Plan. This plan embraced six years of elementary-school training (instead of eight under the older system), four years of "junior high school" (replacing the last two years of elementary school and the first two years of high school), and four years of "junior college" (replacing the last two years of high school and first two of college). Thus, to the slight bewilderment of the uninitiated, there does not exist in Pasadena's school system's nomenclature the term "high school." But the system added two years of college training at public expense.

Mr. Goslin liked, too, the community as he found it developing, a community rich in human resources and rich in material resources, both so necessary, in an educator's opinion, to a modern educational system. Last of all, Mr. Goslin liked what he called Pasadena's "ferment" and spirit of growth and change: he did not need to be told that the old order was still there, but he thought he could discern a new order on the rise, bringing with it the stimulation of new and challenging problems.

Mr. Goslin got back to Minneapolis the second week in April to find a letter on his desk from Vernon Brydolf. It was dated April 2, 1948, and it got down to business at once: "We held a meeting of the Pasadena Board of Education this afternoon and voted unanimously to offer you the regular four-year contract as Superintendent of Schools at an annual salary of $17,500 plus the regular automobile allowance of $50 per month."

Mr. Brydolf went on to say some things that might have seemed, at the time, like little more than a display of courtesy toward a prospective superintendent, but which later took on much greater significance. "Before taking this action," Mr. Brydolf wrote, "I called a number of people with whom you had talked . . . and several others called me. I asked each one how he or she felt the community would react to paying quite a high salary to the new Superintendent of Schools. [Dr. Sexson's highest salary, paid him for the past few months of his reign, was $1,200 a month.] Everyone, without a single exception, said that if the offer was to be made to you, he would approve of it wholeheartedly. There is no doubt you made a tremendous impression . . . all hoping that you will be our next superintendent. . . . Every member of the Board again expressed an even stronger desire for your acceptance." And then, as a spontaneous symbol of friendship from one sportsman to another, Vernon Brydolf penned a longhand postscript: "Both mountain and ocean fishing should be good in California next August. VB."

There was little time for Mr. Goslin to sit back and ponder. On his desk, or in the offing, were several other attractive propositions, should he make up his mind to quit Minneapolis once and for all. Harvard, Columbia, and New York universities were all considering him for important posts. There was talk of a most interesting educational job under Lucius Clay in Western Germany. And there was also talk that he might even be the next United States Commissioner of Education. All these were appealing to a man of Willard Goslin's fervor and energy. At the same time, his entire training and his whole adult life had been devoted to public education; and his dedication to that cause was deep-rooted and profound. The day he got back to Minneapolis he wrote to each Board member in Pasadena a polite little note promising "a final answer within the next few days."

Five days later he wrote to Vernon Brydolf that he was "close to a decision to accept your offer." In that letter, with customary Goslin candor and a characteristic lack of equivocation, he proceeded to set down, for the Board's benefit, the conditions upon which he would insist if he were to accept the appointment. He knew what he wanted; he had been dealing with Boards for a great many years.

Mr. Goslin divided his letter into five main subjects: (1) his relations with the Board; (2) his Administration (a word commonly used to denote a superintendent and his staff); (3) his own role, and how he should spend his time; (4) the superintendent's immediate staff, and (5) the "professional personnel," that is, the teachers.

First of all, wrote Mr. Goslin, it "should be understood that the responsibility and authority for the program of public education rests with the Board of Education as a Board. . . . If I come to Pasadena . . . I will deal with you as a Board and not as individuals so far as the management of the schools is concerned." The Administration would "accept the responsibility for analysis and evaluation of the various matters to be presented to the Board, and with the exception of those items presented only for the information of the Board, would make out presentations in terms of specific recommendations." In other words, Mr. Goslin made it plain that the superintendent and, through him, his staff, would be responsible for administering the affairs of the school community; and, furthermore, that he would not feel an obligation to discuss matters with the Board until he was ready with something definite to recommend. This was, in Mr. Goslin's world, standard operating procedure. But it was a procedure too often disregarded in practice, or too often a subject of complaint by Board members who became irritated at not "being consulted in advance."

It was evident to anyone who studied Mr. Goslin's letter that he was in no sense attempting to withhold from the Board any prerogatives that rightfully belonged to it: the Board still retained its important right of review and of acquiescence; still retained its right to veto, its right to pass on the budget, and accept or reject any Administration recommendation for hiring, firing, or shifting anybody in the entire system. So far as the Pasadena system was concerned, that April day in 1948 when Mr. Goslin wrote his letter, it is quite possible that he, and he alone, saw the need for the explicit stipulations he set down. To any casual reader, they might have sounded somewhat academic. Eventually, however, it was to appear plain to many an educator why a man of Willard Goslin's experience wrote what he did.

Some other conditions laid down in Mr. Goslin's letter were, to him, equally important. He was all for making Board meetings public "with the exception of rare occasions when an executive session is needed. . . ." His time would, he said, be at his own disposal, with "responsibilities" falling in this order: to Pasadena's public schools; to public education in California and the nation; and "to such general citizenship responsibilities as fall to the lot of an individual in a position of leadership in this country." Thus did Mr. Goslin early proclaim, without false modesty, his thesis that a superintendent of schools is a leader not only of the schools, but of the community as a whole.

Mr. Goslin also had some things to say about the people he wanted to work with him. He would "want to multiply my own hands as extensively as possible through the use of at least two assistants attached directly to my office." One of these, he said, would be an educational assistant he expected to bring with him, "an outstanding young woman from the Minneapolis school system who is now connected with my office in a similar capacity." And, because "education can be only as good as the quality of the personality and the extent of the training, experience, and enthusiasm of the professional staff of the school system," he stated emphatically that he would import to Pasadena "the outstanding people in the teaching profession in the United States." Last of all, he warned the Board that, although he was "generally well impressed" with the "sampling" of individuals he had met in Pasadena's system, he would expect the Board of Education "to support me in such adjustments as would from time to time be necessary."

If any member of Pasadena's Board of Education was surprised at Mr. Goslin's plain talk, or objected to what he was asking for, no one bothered to speak up. Indeed, the reaction to Mr. Goslin's letter was one of unmitigated delight; and on the very day it arrived, the Board met and accepted his proposals. That night Mr. Brydolf wrote to Mr. Goslin a most cheerful reply, saying that he and his confreres were "heartily in accord with practically everything you have set forth." The only matters left open for future discussion were of no consequence, such as whether the Board should buy Mr. Goslin a car, as he had asked it to do, or whether they should pay him a monthly allowance for one, which had been its practice in the past.

Mr. Brydolf's letter was dated April 21. That same day Mr. Goslin submitted, in a long, thoughtful, and utterly realistic letter, his resignation as superintendent of schools in Minneapolis. As a letter of resignation, it probably was soon forgotten; as a plain-speaking document, setting forth the beliefs, feelings, criticisms, and philosophies of an outstanding educator, it could easily assume at least a minor place in the archives of important public statements. That which was uppermost in his mind, and in his heart, was contained in one blunt paragraph. "I cannot lend myself any longer," Mr. Goslin wrote, "to the neglect and mistreatment of public education which continues in Minneapolis. This nation literally has its back to the wall and cannot survive as a free people unless the American public will undergird themselves and their ideals with a sound program of public education. The citizens of this community, like the citizens of some other communities, are undermining the institutions and freedom of our country by refusing to support public education in anything like an adequate fashion."

Eight days later it was announced simultaneously in Pasadena and Minneapolis that Willard Edward Goslin had accepted Pasadena's offer to be that city's next superintendent of schools. At once a flood of letters poured in. They were the usual expressions of congratulations, of regret, of well-wishing. But through a great many ran a note of apology, a sense of shame that somehow they, the citizens of Minneapolis, had let a good man down.

4

Mr. Goslin Surveys His Job

Willard Goslin arrived in Pasadena with his wife and second daughter Jane on July 25. They rented a one-story furnished house on the outskirts of town not far from East Orange Grove Avenue (on which they were eventually to live). Mrs. Goslin set about being a superintendent's hospitable wife, and the new superintendent himself set out to have a long and better look at his school system.

There was much work to be done. Having recently gone through a debilitating war, and having been operated under one man's rule for twenty years, the system was, understandably, beginning to run down. By 1948 the postwar period of reconstruction was well under way, and Pasadena's schools were ripe for it. The only new buildings to go up since the war, and for many years before that, were two junior high schools, recently finished and both still to be opened. They would, he knew, present problems of reallocation of students, an especially touchy matter in view of the recent rise in nonwhite pupils. New elementary schools were badly needed to absorb the recent and rapid increase in enrollment, and that meant raising the money to build them. The older buildings in the system were not antiquated compared to many of those in other parts of the country, but even so, Mr. Goslin discovered, they needed such new appurtenances as modern lighting and better seating arrangements.

Mr. Goslin didn't like to admit it aloud, but it was plain to him that the teaching staff itself needed attention. Frictions were at an all-time high—some department heads weren't on speaking terms with subordinates, too many cliques were having free rein, and several departments were functioning as small autocratic entities with, as he put it, "their backs turned and going in opposite directions." Many older administrators were getting ready to retire; that meant replacements in key positions, more of them, Mr. Goslin found out, in the next two years than had been replaced in the last ten. And at the other end of the scale were the probationary teachers—those who had been in the system less than three years. One-third of Pasadena's teachers were in this category, and they all had to be evaluated in the next year.

When he had come West in March, Mr. Goslin had met the three men who would work closely with him in the Central Office. There was Courtenay Monsen, the secretary of the Board of Education, a bespectacled, patient man who had already been there twenty years. He was proud of his impartiality, and proud that he could claim he had never made an enemy among the staff. There was Drummond McCunn, the assistant superintendent in charge of Business Affairs. Mr. McCunn was big and bluff and two-fisted. He was soon to be president of the Tournament of Roses, and had a wide variety of good friends among downtown Pasadenans. And there was Dr. George Merideth, the deputy superintendent whom Willard Goslin had known years before.

Dr. Merideth had been in the system for twenty years, and for many of those years he had been Superintendent Sexson's deputy. He had known the ropes, and was able to handle all sorts of situations his boss had sent his way. But Willard Goslin was not to be so fortunate. George Merideth died of cancer six weeks before Mr. Goslin took office in Pasadena.

His death left the new superintendent with a sticky decision: whether or not to replace him, and if so, with whom. To bring in an outside man at this stage, when he himself was so new, would be just as risky as to elevate someone from within the system about whom he could know but little. The decision Mr. Goslin arrived at was "to live with the situation for several months" without replacing Merideth at all. As it turned out, Mr. Goslin lived with the situation for a full year.

Meanwhile he went about his task with the confidence of a man who knew what he wanted to do—and the first thing he wanted to do was to see his Board of Education in operation. Two days after he arrived in Pasadena, just before he was to start on the relentless round of what he grimly called the "knife and fork circuit"—of breakfast at the Playhouse and lunch with the Chamber of Commerce, of chicken dinners with the Lions, Rotarians, Kiwanians, Optimists, women's leagues, and civic clubs—Willard Goslin went to his first Board meeting. These were the people, these were the five duly elected citizens of Pasadena, with whom he was to work out the educational destiny of some 30,000 students.

5

The Board of Education

There is no such thing as a perfect Board of Education. Because they are human beings elected by other human beings, members of a school Board are exposed to the same desires, frailties, pressures, prejudices, and shortcomings to which people everywhere are exposed. Sometimes—and sometimes too often—members get the idea that they are elected to represent special groups—big business or small business; property owners; schoolteachers; the colored or the white; the Right or the Left. The closest thing to a perfect Board is one made up of men and women who, whatever their private occupations, realize that they represent the community as a whole—big and little business, property owners, and those who merely rent, teachers not as teachers but as citizens, the colored and the white, the Right and the Left. A Board should, ideally, be responsible to all and answerable to none.

It is obvious that the responsibility for selecting a good Board rests with the voters of a community. They must guard against gathering together a group of men and women who, no matter how honest and well meaning and faithful they may be, turn out to be a collective mediocrity; for it is mediocrity in any institution that makes it susceptible to outside influences, just as a man who is physically run down is most susceptible to disease. Lamentably, however, it is a fact that a great many people, and far too many parents, pay little or no attention to the composition or activities of their Boards of Education from one end of the year to the other. Unless they are aroused—and they seldom are—qualified voters at election time stay away from the polls in profuse numbers. Through such professional organizations as the National Education Association and the American Council on Education, through the now widespread promotional work of the National Citizens Commission for the Public Schools, an awakening of interest among responsible citizens has increased since the war. But even so, that interest seldom penetrates to the level of local Board members, whose names and faces not many people know.

The Pasadena Board of Education meets in regular session every Tuesday afternoon at four-thirty. Each member is paid $10 for each session. The Board's conference room, with its unflattering flood of fluorescent lighting, is on the second floor of the Administration Building at 351 South Hudson Avenue, across the street from Bullock's. The five Board members sit on a raised platform at one end of the room behind a highly polished semicircular table. The name of each member, in neat block lettering, stands before him for all in the room to stare at.

It is in this room and at this table that most of the Board's activities and all of its official business are carried on. It is hard work, and many of the meetings are routine and dull. Members must plod through lengthy reports on building construction, on finances, on purchases and expenditures. They must pass on every employee when he is hired, fired, or simply shifted from one job to another. They must decide on new school sites, and condemn them in time to protect the public pocketbook. They must pass on the three budgets for the three districts in Pasadena's schools—elementary, junior high, and junior college. They must listen to any Pasadena citizen, composed or irate, whenever he comes to argue or agree, complain or praise.

Willard Goslin sat in the conference room at 351 South Hudson Avenue practically every week for two and a half years. Despite his trips out of town, he missed no more than three or four meetings in all that time. And, in all that time, there was only one change in the Board's membership. One year after Mr. Goslin's arrival, William L. Blair, the associate editor of the Pasadena *Star-News*, chose not to run for reelection after twenty consecutive years on the Board. Although it had been his inflexible policy never to write about Board affairs in his newspaper column, he had served his city and his system conservatively and well, with competence and force. His year with Mr. Goslin as superintendent had been constructive and peaceful, and his retirement, acknowledged by a handsome gold pen and pencil set given him by the Board, was unanimously regretted.

As the Board was subsequently constituted, its oldest member in point of service was Vernon M. Brydolf, the local attorney who was its president when Willard Goslin came into office. As the father of three now-grown children who had gone through the city's schools, Vernon Brydolf has had personal as well as professional interest in his job and the schools. This spring he rounds out his fourteenth year as a member, and still has two more years to serve. He looks and acts like the solid Pasadena citizen he is: short and heavy-set, rather slow and deliberate. The fine quality of his voice gives the impression that he would make an impressive trial lawyer, had he not chosen instead a civil practice. His civic contributions to Pasadena have been considerable: he is an erstwhile president of its Bar Association, four times president of its Community Chest, a campaign chairman of the War Chest, a member of the board of the Pasadena Art Institute, and a most active member of the Optimists Club. He is Pasadena's counterpart of good, honest, sincere citizenship to be found everywhere in the land.

Next to Vernon Brydolf, Mrs. Gladys Cummings Rinehart has sat on the Board longer than anyone else. Moreover her ten years there were preceded by a very active interest in public schools. She taught in Pasadena more than thirty years ago, when she first came to town with her father and seven brothers. After she got married and her two children started kindergarten, she joined the Parent-Teachers Association. Soon she was president of her local chapter, and before her children had grown up she had gone on to the peak job in local PTA affairs: the presidency of Pasadena's important PTA Council, representing some thirty districts in the community. Now her children are married and she has two grandchildren. Her husband, a successful lawyer, is a 33rd-degree Scottish Mason, and Gladys Rinehart's one hobby continues to be public education. Although Mrs. Rinehart has a charmingly vague way of expressing herself, and is exceedingly bad at remembering dates and the sequence of events, these characteristics are deceiving. Beneath the slightly Zasu Pitts mannerisms, there lies a penetrating knowledge of school affairs and an unswerving devotion to any cause she thinks is right. One day Willard Goslin was to find her a fast and loyal friend.

Mrs. Rinehart's feminine cohort on the Board, Miss Harriet Sterling, is a determined woman of mature years, and a lifelong Democrat. For more than a decade she taught English in Pasadena's public schools, and for twelve years she was head of a high-school English department in the system. A few years ago she had a serious eye operation which almost lost her the sight of one eye. After that Miss Sterling retired from the school system —and, she thought, from any more connection with it except for contact with those teachers who were her friends. In the winter of 1947, however, a group of teachers who, like some of their companions, were unhappy with the John Sexson régime, came to their friend Harriet Sterling and asked her if she would run for the school Board. No one could have been more surprised, and at first she said No. Since her operation Miss Sterling had been leading a very quiet, undisturbed life. She and a friend shared a small bungalow-type house, cheery and neat with well pressed antimacassars on its comfortable chairs, and she was finding it none too easy to get about. Today, even with her bad eye somewhat improved, she says she has not read a book in six years. The teachers were insistent, however, and, finally, since the job attracted her as a means of occupying herself, Harriet Sterling accepted. And as she reflects back, with some relish, on her campaign and election, she is proud that she was put up by teachers and proud that they helped elect her. "The teachers were my friends then," she says firmly, "and they are now."

Miss Sterling's running mate in the 1947 election was Milton Wopschall. He was then only twenty-eight years old, the youngest member to be elected to the Board in a long time. He has lived in Pasadena since he was four and went through its public schools. During the war, after being turned down by the Navy because of flat feet, he ended up, ironically enough, in the Infantry, in a desk job that kept him from overseas duty. He completed an interrupted college career by graduating in 1942 from the School of Administration at the University of Southern California, married a local girl, became the father of three children, and is now secretary and treasurer of his father's wholesale and retail paint business, the largest of its kind in town. When he ran for the Board, it was persistently rumored that he also was a teachers' candidate, put up to get Dr. Sexson out, but this Milton Wopschall denies. Although he did, eventually, vote not to renew the Sexson contract, he maintains that he was put up by some friends he went to school with, and "ran to improve business procedure in the system." When discussing the paint business, he is relaxed and knowing; when discussing school Board affairs he often talks hesitantly, creating the impression of uncertainty, blinking his eyes as if the lights were bothering him. While discussing a controversial problem, he has a habit of tearing up scraps of paper with infinite care.

The fifth man on the Board, elected when William Blair retired, is a handsome and spirited undertaker named Lawrence C. Lamb. His campaign was a relatively lively one, because among the eleven candidates running were two people whom the most conservative members of the community suspected of Socialist leanings. As the newest member to be elected, and comparatively unknown, he ran behind Vernon Brydolf and Gladys Rinehart, and beat out the next highest by only 194 votes. Lawrence Lamb appears much younger than his forty-four years. His curly brown hair is close-cropped, his skin is smooth and clear and has a well massaged look. His sudden smile displays an excellent set of teeth. A short, muscular individual, he is in excellent trim as a result of horseback riding and chores on the Lamb ranch outside Pasadena. For years they kept a cow there, and Lawrence Lamb used to milk it daily. "I have," says he, "a sort of pastoral background." Like his colleague, Milton Wopschall, he attended Pasadena schools. He spent one year at Pasadena City College, and then got married, for the first time, when he was twenty. The marriage was a quick failure, and soon thereafter Mr. Lamb remarried, most happily. He has a son by his first marriage, three children by his second, and is raising a son his present wife had by a former husband who died. Once Mr. Lamb was chairman of the Board of Trustees of Pasadena's Tremont Baptist Church, and he still sings bass in its choir. "Religion," says he, "is my flora and fauna."

The Lamb Funeral Home is on East Orange Grove Avenue, on the edge of a middle-class residential district. Lawrence Lamb and his brother John inherited it from their father and they operate it as a partnership which nets Lawrence about $25,000 a year. It is only because he makes that much a year, he says with frankness, that he feels he can afford to be on the school Board, a subject on which he is voluble and outspoken. "A Board member has to take a big gamble when he puts up his name to run," he says. "And after you get elected, people try to divorce you from what is naturally yours. A person running for the Board has to have a sense of humor. He runs an awful chance of having his name smirched, and I can't afford that, because I have sixteen or eighteen people working for me in the business—I've an ambulance service, a crematory, and a mortician business. That means forty or fifty mouths to feed, and I'm entirely dependent on the good-will of the people."

Mr. Lamb is equally clear about the responsibilities of the Pasadena Board of Education: "We are not charged with keeping a national figure here; we are not charged with promoting a national program of any type of education; we are not charged with supporting Federal aid, or many of the other concepts current in education. We are charged with the welfare of our local school system and its interests. That's foremost in our minds. I don't say all those national things are bad. They just aren't our responsibilities."

Willard Goslin was not to meet Lawrence Lamb for a year. But he sat down with the others, that July afternoon in 1948, in an atmosphere of amiable good-will and friendliness. He told them he did not then want to say anything, but that he was glad to be there. They replied that they were glad to have him. Then everyone settled down to the year's work.

6

The Honeymoon

The least of Willard Goslin's worries, that first summer, was the budget. It had been prepared by the previous Administration, was almost in final form, and was approved soon after he took office. The financial problem needing attention was the forthcoming $5,000,000 bond issue to raise money for new elementary schools. Soon after taking office Mr. Goslin talked the matter over with the Board, pointing out that there hadn't been any new construction to speak of since the thirties, and asking the Board to draw up a resolution calling for a bond election on October 1, six weeks away. Next day the Board got together with Mr. Goslin and other Administration officials at the University Club for a full-dress discussion of the election. A week later the resolution setting the date was duly passed.

Mr. Goslin's honeymoon with his Board lasted for a long time. When he presented to the Board the names of the two women he had told them, in his first letter, he would bring to Pasadena, the Board approved both appointments with alacrity. Miss Mary Beauchamp, the "outstanding young woman" he brought from Minneapolis to be his educational assistant, was to get a flat $4,500 for a ten-month year; Mrs. Karol Greeson, a widow who had once worked for him in Webster Groves, was to be paid $400 a month. His only other administrative appointment that fall, also approved without reservation, was that of young Franklin K. Patterson, a teacher in a local secondary school, to a part-time job as Assistant Secondary (school) Curriculum Coordinator.

Most of the Board meetings for the balance of 1948 were routine, and in the main Mr. Goslin busied himself with his staff. His schedule was full, and he was full of plans. By the end of the year he had presented the Board with two proposals of some moment, and they were followed, early in the new year, by many others.

The first of the two year-end proposals, although it had little effect on education, was significant because it illustrated the importance the new superintendent attached to Board meetings themselves. Up to this time minutes of meetings had been so brief, so sketchy, that they were of almost no value as a source of reference. Mr. Goslin explained to the Board that he and Board Secretary Courtenay Monsen, who was in charge of keeping the minutes, had been working on a plan to revise them and extend them to a point where, when a general discussion took place in meeting, they would be written up in great detail. Minutes that once covered only five or six pages now would cover some twenty or thirty. Toward that end, Mr. Goslin said, a stenographic report would be made of discussions at each meeting. The proposal was warmly welcomed by the Board.

The second recommendation was of more general interest. In mid-December, following up a letter he had written to the Board about the matter, Mr. Goslin suggested that Pasadena eliminate entirely the promotion of students at midyear, and place all promotions on an annual basis. He pointed out that the transition, necessarily a gradual one, had been taking place in some schools in the community for quite a while, and that now there remained approximately 1,500 students still to make the change. Annual promotions were, as the Board knew, the rule in other parts of the country. It was less upsetting to schedule making, and it meant that children stayed with the same teacher for a longer time, which was good for morale and for guidance. Mr. Goslin said that he had checked with his elementary-school principals, and that they reported they had prepared the community for the shift, through their PTA's and other parent groups. Perhaps the biggest single group to feel the shock of the move, Mr. Goslin warned, would be parents of children who were ready to go to kindergarten or enter the first grade next February: their children would have to stay home, or go to preschool classes, until next September. During the meeting, Board members centered their discussion mainly around the timing of the move, with Mr. Blair commenting that it might have been better to have made such an announcement the previous September. However, the motion for the shift was that day presented, seconded, and approved.

On January 25, 1949—six months to the day after he took office—Willard Goslin was ready to lay before the Board some of the projects and plans he had in mind for the city's schools.

First he outlined his plans for what he termed "vertical group" discussions. To anyone unfamiliar with modern educational jargon, talk of a "vertical group" is likely to conjure up all sorts of dreadful, dangerous, not to mention subversive, scholastic activity. But if, as they listened to Mr. Goslin, the Board members harbored any such ideas, they didn't bat an eye.

Actually, a vertical group, as applied to a school system and as Mr. Goslin was using the term, is simply an organization that embraces all levels of a staff, from top to bottom, as opposed to the somewhat antiquated system of freezing all contact activity at a horizonal level, where interplay and exchange of ideas and thoughts and experience—in other words, communication—between members of, say, elementary schools and junior colleges, would be kept to an intolerable minimum. To most laymen, such vertical group activity might have seemed too academic and too professional for their understanding. To the educator, it meant a great deal; it might even mean the difference between a successful teaching program and an unsuccessful one.

Mr. Goslin planned, he told the Board, to establish in the system some fifty-odd groups of men and women, each containing some twenty or thirty people, who would meet periodically for some six months, on school (working) time. Each group would be as mixed a conglomeration of individuals as card-shuffling IBM machines could shuffle them: the names of everyone from telephone operators and janitors to principals and supervisors would be run through, and come out assigned to a group. To lead these verticals Mr. Goslin proposed to select some sixty-odd teachers and administrators in the system, who would meet with him, as superintendent, at a series of pre-training sessions.

Next Mr. Goslin looked ahead to the following summer. During vacation time, he told the Board, he would like to start the first of a series of summer workshops. As possibly some Board members did not know, there was nothing new or radical about summer workshops in public education in the United States. They came into being some ten years ago as an outgrowth of a voluminous eight-year study of secondary education in thirty schools, a study costing over a million dollars and made in cooperation with practically every college and university in the United States. Now a number of school systems operate summer workshops as a regular part of in-service teacher training, and they are no longer considered experimental. Their essential function is to bring teachers together for concerted study and research outside the classroom. They bring unity into a system, educators believe, the way nothing else does. Teachers haven't the time to discuss their problems with each other during the school year; they haven't even the time to get to know their fellows, professionally, as well as they should. And, valuable though they are, courses at a university are not the same thing, lacking as they do both the intimate daily contact with others studying the same problems, and the broadness of a workshop's base.

As outlined to the Board, Mr. Goslin's program—with its lectures, its panel of visiting experts in teacher training, its discussion groups, and its free afternoon periods for such time-consuming (and necessary) chores as previewing educational films—was to be open to all the administrative and teaching staffs of the Pasadena schools. The workshop would run for five weeks, and attendance would be optional.

Mr. Goslin went into these plans thoroughly because he set great store by them. What he hoped these conferences and meetings would add up to would be the beginning of a program having as its objective the welding of all the intellectual forces of the Pasadena school system into a sound scholastic unit. The only program of value, he has always stressed, is one that takes effect in the mind of the teacher. And his was not a program that could be welded in a week or a month or a year. Indeed, it was a never ending program; and its results were only to be measured eventually by the worth of its end product: the worth of the students it turned out. Again, if any reservations regarding these plans were felt by any member of the Board, they were not indicated.

At another Board meeting two weeks after his talk on January 25, Mr. Goslin reported on enrollment for the second semester (another increase—up 344—in elementary; another increase—up 110—in junior high), and brought up the fact that in the proposed calendar for the 1949–1950 school year, two days had been added to the students' school time: a total of 177 days. For this reason, and because he thought orientation and refresher courses were good for teachers, he thought teachers should be called back a week early, the next September, with extra pay. With California tending to have the shortest school day, in number of minutes, in the United States, teachers hadn't, in Mr. Goslin's opinion, enough time to complete required work, and needed a more leisurely and calmer approach to their job. In reply, Mr. Wopschall rather dryly observed that he thought much instructional time was being lost owing to interruptions for assemblies and extracurricular activities scheduled during the teaching day. But he voiced no real objection to the idea, and Mr. Brydolf expressed his approval. Since it was not put in the form of a proposal, however, the suggestion was not then voted upon.

At several subsequent Board meetings another matter was aired that obviously was disturbing some members of the Board. This had to do with information leaking to the press before it was given to the Board. One week Milton Wopschall voiced his concern over the fact that he had learned of various matters only by reading about them in the papers. A week later

Miss Sterling voiced her disapproval of learning in the same way about people being hired before their names had been brought up in meeting—and, as a former teacher, she may have felt that matters of hiring were her special concern. Mr. Goslin replied that he, too, was disturbed when news leaked, and determined to do his best to discover the cause and stop it at its source. As for personnel, however, he explained that, to forestall much-sought-after teachers being grabbed up by another school system, they were sometimes secured quietly, before their names were presented to the Board; but that such appointments were, of course, tentative, and subject to Board approval. The discussion ended by the Board's expressing confidence both in the superintendent and in the personnel office.

As Mr. Goslin's régime shifted into high gear, many other subjects came up before the Board and were harmoniously disposed of. They ranged all the way from a debate on when the classrooms should be repainted to criticism by Businessman Wopschall of the money-losing cafeterias. As they always are, a number of letters were received and filed—letters from PTA's concerning local school projects, letters concerning recreation activities, letters complaining about lighting in the schools, letters thanking Mr. Goslin for speeches he had made, letters on every conceivable subject, including, on March 26, one from the Property Owners Division saying that at its February meeting it had been resolved, moved, and passed that the Board of Education be urged to curtail expenditures in its 1949–1950 budget.

In June, as Mr. Goslin's first year in Pasadena drew to a close, the system had its biennial school Board election, and Lawrence C. Lamb, the mortician, was elected to replace retiring William Blair.

One week before he was to take office, Mr. Lamb appeared at a Board meeting as a citizen of Altadena, and rose to say that he wished to register his objection to the proposed size of a new gymnasium soon to be built at the Eliot Junior High School. After Mr. Lamb voiced his objections to the gymnasium's size, Mr. Wopschall suggested that action on the matter be postponed until the following week, so that Citizen Lamb, by then Board Member Lamb, could vote his objection. But Mr. Lamb said No. In fact, he specifically asked that the Board reach its decision at this meeting. He was, he explained, "merely a spokesman," and did not intend to interfere in any way with the Board's decision after he had taken office. All in all, this apparent hedging struck some of those present as strange and bewildering.

Behind Willard Goslin, as he rounded out his first twelve months in Pasadena, lay a year of peaceful, harmonious relations with his Board. There was no reason for him to believe, at this time, that such conditions would not prevail indefinitely. And for the Board's part, it seemed satisfied that it was getting the forward-looking kind of program it had so badly wanted when it offered Mr. Goslin the job a little over a year before.

7

Some Errors, Some Runs, Some Hits

When Dr. John Sexson was superintendent of Pasadena's schools, he was a popular exponent of what might be called the Open Door Policy of administration, especially during the last few years of his long reign. The Open Door Policy simply meant that he was available for interviews and appointments and general conversation to most of the people most of the time. This endeared him to a great many citizens.

The arrival of Willard Goslin caused a change in this policy as sudden and, to some people, as shocking, as though a door had been literally slammed in their faces. Before he had been in town a week, the story had got around that you couldn't see the new superintendent without making an appointment, and that sometimes you couldn't see him until the next week at that. Essentially the story was quite accurate. But behind it lay another story, a story that took some of those citizens a good two or three years to understand.

In twenty-five years as a school superintendent, Willard Goslin had developed a method of operation that differed radically from Dr. Sexson's. He did not like glad-handing and did not enjoy sociability for its own sake. His broadly based concepts of an educator's role in the community did not include the customarily accepted idea that special groups, especially business interests, should be catered to. The cynical maxim "Policy is the best policy" was foreign to his nature.

In Pasadena, Mr. Goslin saw no reason to change his ways. For one thing, he had a tremendous amount of work to do, with more demands on his time than there were hours in the day to take care of them, and with no right hand, like Dr. Meredith, who had been on the scene for years and, as an established part of the school administration, could have assumed some of the superintendent's load. There was, for example, that $5,000,000 bond-issue election to be run off in October—a comparatively simple idea to sell the public, it is true, since a bond issue does not directly affect a citizen's pocketbook, but a matter nevertheless demanding much of a superintendent's time and energy. The bond issue was a success: the vote was over four-to-one in favor. Meanwhile, Mr. Goslin was plunging into the business of administrating some 1,200 principals, supervisors, and teachers, of overseeing an $8,500,000 annual outlay, and of beginning the spadework for revivifying an educational system and modernizing and expanding an educational plant. All this work, moreover, had to be accomplished when he was not out of town, serving as president of the American Association of School Administrators.

It is quite likely that Willard Goslin could not have changed his method of doing business had he wanted to. Again, it simply was not in his nature, a nature which has always consisted of a combination of paradoxes. He has long been considered to be one of the top educators in the country, and yet he has never taken his Ph.D. He is rated an intellectual by many, and yet he has never been a great student of the classics and could never be described as a scholar. As a public speaker he is almost without parallel, and yet he has never prepared a speech before giving it.

Even his appearance is contradictory. He is six feet one and, because he is lean and hard and fit, he looks taller. His silver-gray hair is close-cropped at the sides, his eyes are a light gray-green, his smile is slow and engaging. His resemblance to Will Rogers is startling—the thin, rather bony face, the grin, the forelock, the slight ducking of the head, even the pleasant, quiet drawl, and the frequent use of the homely phrase. He is a man of real humility and honesty, but he lacks false modesty, and he gives the impression that he is quite sure he can and should play a leading role in education in the United States. His simplicity, his unassuming approach to anything he tackles, can be disarming: he is a man of dogged determination. He is a man with a mission.

And as a man with a mission, Mr. Goslin conducted his administration in his own highly individual way. Some critics might not have admired him as an administrator because he was not strong on detail. But that was not his idea of what a good administrator should be. He picked his staff with care, and when anyone was assigned a job Mr. Goslin expected him to follow through without interference from above. On matters of any educational consequence, the superintendent was thorough and completely competent. Because he seemed to feel more at home and at ease with a group rather than with individual staff members, he often discussed important matters with more than one person. This policy had two conflicting effects: any group he was talking to felt a great respect and admiration for him and a lively appreciation of what he was talking about, but at the same time some individuals in the system who never got to know him had the feeling that here was a man who was distant and not very friendly. He was, then, an inspirational leader for many men rather than a close confidant of any one man. It was a strength, and a weakness.

Mr. Goslin went about his business in Pasadena with an honest disdain for the petty jealousies and annoyances that soon began a slow boil about him. His tight schedule of office appointments, his frequent trips out of town, his refusal to lunch often at the University Club when he *was* in town, the protective wall around him established by a zealous and loyal office staff, his inability to backslap, salve small egos, or play the political game fast and loose, caused resentment among people who were accustomed to an informal régime, and who could not or would not understand what he was driving at.

Of more immediate consequence was the new superintendent's attitude toward the press. In Minneapolis he had never put on a hail-fellow-well-met act for the newspaper boys, but had nevertheless gained and held the respect and admirataion of practically all of them. When Mr. Goslin got to Pasadena and met its new problems, he saw, in this regard also, no reason to alter his attitude. That, to him, would have been bootlicking. He held a press conference on his first preappointment inspection visit, and it was highly successful. Those present went away singing his praises. After he came back and set up his office, he held another. Then he got down to work, and the press was treated like everyone else—courteously, but through appointments. This so enraged a reporter for the *Star-News* who had been covering the education beat for years that he finally gave up trying to see the superintendent at all, wrote practically nothing about him personally, and reported school news without benefit of the superintendent's advice and help. As a weapon for those who seized on anything that would tend to point up the superintendent as an unfriendly, uncooperative man, the reporter's antagonism later came in handy. And it was an inescapable indication of the Goslin Administration's poorly conceived public-relations program, which was one day to give him so much trouble.

For entirely other reasons, the appointment of Mary Beauchamp, the woman from Minneapolis, as Mr. Goslin's educational assistant, also had unfortunate results. In that same capacity in Minneapolis, Mary Beauchamp, who no one guessed was thirty-seven years old, had had the regard and cooperation of all those who worked with her: she was fast-thinking and smart, a demon for work; and she was accepted as an important member of a team of forward-looking educators. She had previously taught school and was working toward her Doctor's degree when her boss brought her to Pasadena as part of the administrative set-up he had outlined to Vernon Brydolf. In Pasadena she was completely unknown and alone, "about as big," Mr. Goslin once described her, "as a cake of soap after two days' use." She at once took up in the job she had handled so successfully in Minneapolis, and at once she ran into trouble. Without a deputy superintendent, Mr. Goslin automatically turned over to her some details of his job she already knew how to handle. When he was out of town, educational matters at the superintendent level were referred to her, and she dealt with them, as she always had, with sharpness, decision, and dispatch.

But some of those she had to deal with—especially a few of the Central Office staff who, before the arrival of Mr. Goslin, had had hopes for their own advancement—resented her being there. They resented her because she had been given authority which they thought she took advantage of; they resented her because she was a very feminine person who looked much younger than she was; they resented her because they knew that, educationally, she thought as Willard Goslin thought, believing in a reasonably decentralized administration and in the necessity for taking a strong stand on controversial issues like rezoning.

Although she eventually came to be respected and liked by many of the system's staff with whom she worked, some of those who originally objected to her never became her friends. At least one incident stood out as a mistake that was, by her own admission, real and unfortunate. Once, while the superintendent was out of town, an assistant principal of a junior high school had created a mild (and unpublicized) local furor by slapping a student. Telephone complaints began coming through to one of Mr. Goslin's secretaries. When the calls got out of hand, Miss Beauchamp was asked to take over. She asked the school's principal, never a Goslin friend, to come to see her and discuss the matter with her and a few others of the Central Office staff. He did so, and explained the incident by saying that his assistant's patience had "worn thin." Miss Beauchamp thereupon remarked that patiences should not wear thin, and that the student should have been treated with greater care. The principal never forgave Mary Beauchamp for giving him what he considered a dressing-down in front of others.

In March of 1950, Miss Beauchamp was offered an opportunity she had long wanted—to teach at New York University while she worked toward her doctoral degree. After talking it over with Mr. Goslin and others, she accepted it and handed in her resignation, to become effective in July. While she was in Pasadena she gave many evidences of having performed most of her tasks well, and her leaving had nothing to do with whatever errors in judgment she might have made in a difficult spot. But because she was so closely identified with the Goslin Administration and the Goslin educational program, she continued to be a target, even after she left, for those who were looking for a chance to criticize the kind of job Willard Goslin was doing.

In the meantime Mr. Goslin was concentrating on his job, not looking for trouble and not listening to gossip; his time was fully occupied with essentials. After the October, 1948, bond election was out of the way, he was beset with the task of putting together an organization for the new elementary-school construction about to begin. He had found, to his surprise, that no such organization existed—no engineer, for example, and no adequate staff of draftsmen. He went out and hired them. He could find no school census and no detailed breakdown of school population, so necessary when deciding upon where to build the new schools. He had one made. One of his most difficult chores was the choosing and obtaining of suitable sites. It is a paradoxical fact that while everyone wants public schools, no one wants one close to home.

As his dealings with the School Board testified, Mr. Goslin went slowly when it came to new appointments. The old schoolroom adage that a new broom always sweeps clean is an ironic distortion of the facts when it comes to a school system itself. So far as the principals, supervisors, and teachers were concerned, a new superintendent could not have swept clean had he wanted to. Although there were some notoriously weak spots, and, as has already been observed, many men and women were fast approaching retirement, tenure protected them. Where Mr. Goslin could have used his broom ruthlessly—again, had he wanted to—was in the Central Administrative Office, with its three departments: the superintendent's office itself, the Department of Instructional Service, and the Department of Business Service. But Mr. Goslin did not want to, as is evidenced by a progress report issued over two years after he had taken office. This report listed staff assignments as they stood at the end of Dr. Sexson's stay, and as they were as of November, 1950. When, a few days after the report was issued, the educational crisis burst like a bomb over the city, the cry went out that Willard Goslin had "tried to go too far too fast." But the cold statistics and blunt facts in the report, which so few people bothered to read, eloquently told a different story.

Of the forty-three persons on the Central Office payroll in July, 1948, only eleven had been replaced by Willard Goslin. Of those eleven, one was Goslin himself, replacing Sexson; one was a replacement for George Merideth, deceased—a year after Merideth's death; a third was necessitated by Drummond McCunn's resigning as assistant superintendent a year after Mr. Goslin's arrival; and still another replacement, in a minor post, was caused by a death. Of the eleven, only four were the result of Mr. Goslin's shifting people out of the posts they held.

During those same two years, Mr. Goslin made eleven additions to the staff. One of them was the controversial Mary Beauchamp. Another was the superintendent's administrative assistant, Karol Greeson. All of the other "additional positions" were the result of the proven need for more people, caused by the opening of two new junior high schools and increased enrollment. Thus the head supervisor of Arts, at his own request, was given an assistant. The chief physician inspector was given three. A new psychologist was added. And so it went.

Perhaps Willard Goslin's most important appointment was the one he waited a year to make. In July, 1949, he brought into the system an able administrator and educator who had worked for him in Minneapolis: Dr. Robert S. Gilchrist, a big, balding, friendly man from Colorado, who had a Ph.D. and once was a full professor at Ohio State. Although Dr. Gilchrist was listed as a replacement for the late George Merideth, his duties as well as his title were to be different. Called assistant (instead of deputy) superintendent, he was to be responsible for instructional service (in less fancy words that meant teaching and teaching administration), and he was to have nothing to do with the business end of the show. Under him were placed all the teaching services—curriculum, the arts, guidance and counseling, health, vocational education, and, of course, all the schools in the system: twenty-two elementary schools, seven junior highs, and two junior colleges. One of the important Goslin changes Dr. Gilchrist began to implement was the shift of the curriculum department in the Central Office from a horizontal to a vertical organization, so that the department would operate at all levels as a unit. This was a radical departure from the old days when, as Mr. Goslin once said, "You'd just start building one end of the bridge here, and the other there, and hope they'd meet in the middle."

By the close of 1949 Mr. Goslin was ready to make two more important appointments. One was caused by the resignation of Drummond McCunn (somewhat to the satisfaction of both, incidentally), to go to Contra Costa County, and the other was caused by Mr. Goslin's conviction that he needed a new personnel director.

To find a business manager to replace Mr. McCunn, Mr. Goslin looked over the field both in Pasadena and elsewhere. His candidates included several Pasadena principals who had their eyes on the job, and two likely California administrators who did not. He finally picked a thirty-three-year-old counselor at Pasadena City College, Stuart Marsee, who had taken his Master's and Bachelor's degrees in School Administration at the University of Oregon, and had spent three years in the Navy Supply Corps. He was two-fisted, rugged, and redheaded. His appointment was made just a few months before the Goslin forces were to open their campaign for an increase in the school tax levy, hardly a comfortable time for a new man to take over such a job. Dr. Marsee didn't find the going easy. By the time the spring of 1950 had come around, he found himself in the middle of a knock-down fight.

To seek out a new personnel director, Mr. Goslin kept well within the bounds of his school system. He sent a notice to all 1,200 of the system's staff advising them that the job was open, and inviting any candidates to submit their names and qualifications. Forty-one applied, and for some two months a panel of three from the Central Office, including the superintendent, interviewed and sifted and, finally, came up with a recommendation. In April a soft-spoken, hard-working young man named Blair Nixon, an assistant principal at a junior high, was appointed with the unanimous approval of the Board. He was the last appointment of any consequence Willard Goslin was to make.

During the days when these new men were taking over, some muffled mutterings could be heard among the ambitious who had been passed over: the kind of jealousies and disappointments any promotions and shifts are bound to create. If they got to Mr. Goslin's ear, he made no comment. For by now, in the winter of 1950, it was obvious that he was well on his way toward revitalizing Pasadena's school system. The building program was in full swing. His first vertical group conferences had resulted in a long and instructive report. His administrative forces were now established and working as a team. He had appointed a number of committees, in which he had included laymen as well as staff members, to advise on such things as child guidance, conservation, summer camps, probationary teachers; and these had taken him a long step ahead in his plan for bringing the community into the schools. And by this time he had promoted three projects which he considered essential—he had encouraged the use of the already established "core system," he had held his first "convention" of his Central Office staff, and, as he had told the Board he would, he had conducted the system's first summer workshop.

The core system is something that is still the subject of much debate. Some modern educators are convinced it will never work because of the unavailability of properly trained man power, but many others are equally convinced it *must* work because they believe it is fundamental to the proper growth and development of children. The system consists, in essence, of placing a high-school student under the direction of some one teacher for at least two hours (and preferably three) a day, and of having that teacher instruct the student in two or three related subjects during that time. This system, obviously, is a departure from the customary high-school plan of allotting a different teacher to students for each hour of their six-hour day of school work. The core system, many educators believe, not only has the advantage of softening the intellectual shock of a sudden change-over from the student's having one teacher all day (hence all year) in elementary school; it also—and possibly more basically—gives the student a counselor to guide him and direct him in school at a time in his life when he needs it most. Some die-hards have labeled the system superprogressive, in the peculiar belief that it tends to woo the student away from his parents, and have described it as one of the more horrendous "frills" of modern education. But many thorough studies have indicated the soundness, indeed the necessity, of the program.

The strength of the core system could, of course, conceivably be its weakness. A core teacher must be an exceptionally able teacher, and must have special training for the job, or else the student would lose more than he gained. Thus it was that, with regard to expanding the core system, Mr. Goslin moved with caution.

The "convention" was another step toward integration of staff members. Just before school opened in the fall of 1949, Mr. Goslin had asked members of his Central Office force if they would like to spend three days at a holiday resort called Glenn Ranch, at their own expense—three days of tennis and golf and informal talks in the sun, along with more formal meetings to discuss ways and means of improving operations, and to air complaints and listen to suggestions. No one was compelled to go, and there would be no reprisals against those who didn't. Nevertheless, over seventy men and women—90 per cent of the staff—turned up, and pronounced it such a success that they immediately started talking about a return engagement the following year. After the Glenn Ranch Conference was over, its findings were carried into each school by supervisors and curriculum coordinators, and there, in a further series of meetings, the same matters were discussed. In turn, the staff members brought back from the schools reports on problems confronting principals and teachers.

The first summer workshop had also, in the opinion of most of those who attended, been stimulating and worth while as a means of unifying the teaching staff and of supplying them with in-service training. Among the visiting scholars Willard Goslin invited to his workshop that year was a seventy-eight-year-old man from Columbia University, a man who, among modern educational philosophers and students, is known and respected throughout the world. A liberal, a progressive in education, and at all times a controversial figure, William Heard Kilpatrick was brought to Pasadena because the superintendent felt that his key educators would gain a great deal by a week's contact with this man. Twenty-nine of those key people did spend five days listening to Dr. Kilpatrick, sitting with him in informal discussion meetings. They came away, according to well substantiated reports, intellectually refreshed and inspired. Soon, however, word was going around that Kilpatrick was a disciple of old John Dewey, whose name was anathema to many people, and that he was on some lists of organizations suspected of Communistic attachments. In a community as conservative as Pasadena, any reputation Dr. Kilpatrick might have won as a scholar and educator was overshadowed by the allegation that he and other Dewey disciples advanced, especially in their written works, many radical political and economic theories. It might be remembered, however, that these radical theories had been advanced in the thirties, when it was not uncommon for genuine liberals to espouse points of view which they no longer hold.

Before many months had passed, it was being whispered

around Pasadena that Dr. Kilpatrick's five days of lectures were indirectly designed to undermine the native patriotism of Pasdena's youth. By this time the forces which were already beginning to organize against the Goslin Administration were using the name Kilpatrick and the names of other Goslin workshop guests as their most formidable ammunition.

8

The Forces Against

On a series of evenings early in the winter of 1949, a group of citizens got together to discuss education in the Pasadena public schools. The first meeting, attended by about a hundred men and women, was held in the big roomy house of a Mrs. Walter Payne. The second meeting was shifted to a local American Legion hall because the organizers thought more people might show up. More did not—estimates placed the count at about seventy—but those who did were anything but downhearted.

It can be stated with accuracy that most of the people went to these early meetings because they felt that their children were not doing as well in school as they thought they should. There are many and varying reasons why some children do not do well in school, ranging all the way from the fact that this child is not really very bright to the fact that that child has had the bad break of getting a poor teacher. A great deal of research, however, has gone into the subject of child growth and development, and innumerable case histories have been studied and reported upon. Out of them has come the incontrovertible fact that some children don't do well in school because of maladjustments in home life. Oversupervision of children by well intentioned parents sometimes comes about because the parents themselves are restlessly reaching for a higher niche in the social strata and pass this along to their children. And many parents, it seems, are perfectly willing to go to a doctor when their child is sick, but they still feel that education is a personal thing about which no one knows more than they.

Be that as it may, there were some dissatisfied parents in Pasadena, and a group of them got together and called themselves, rather grandly, the School Development Council. But like all such organizations, this one underwent several changes in management and membership as it proceeded on its course. Finally there came a time when even the cause itself seemed to have changed. Some of those who went to early meetings dropped out before long because they felt that the originally stated purpose of the group had been obscured by narrow prejudice and a false set of educational values.

Off and on, the School Development Council's membership was composed of a number of people who, if not exactly the community's leading citizens, were certainly representatives of its main street. Its first chairman was W. Glenn Ebersole, a short, gray-haired man who travels for the Blue Cross Hospital Service. Its second chairman was John C. Petterson, a brisk little man who has blondish hair and a boyish face that belie his fifty-nine years and who owns and operates his own company making partitions and flush doors. He stepped in when his friend Mr. Ebersole found the press of personal affairs too arduous to continue in the job. These two were the entrepreneurs of School Development Council in its early and less active days, although neither had very close school ties. Mr. Ebersole had no children, and Mr. Petterson's only child, a daughter, had not gone to school in Pasadena for many years and by now was grown up and married.

The chief activities of the School Development Council that first year were to put up a candidate for the Board of Education in the spring of 1949 and to protest against certain phases of Mr. Goslin's first budget. The reason for their backing a candidate was to defeat one or both of two people running who, the Council stated emphatically, were "Socialists." (That one of the two they opposed was an attorney with an old and conservative law firm deterred them not at all.) As it turned out, their candidate was defeated (by Lawrence Lamb), but they at least had the satisfaction of knowing that neither of the "Socialists" was elected.

With their first try at budget affairs the School Development Council had better luck. As originally prepared, the 1949–1950 budget contained a proposal to bring back all teachers one week early the following fall so that they could be given some preseason training and discuss the program for the forthcoming term. This would cost $100,000. The School Development Council, after doing some quiet talking around town, wrote a vigorous letter to the Board objecting to it. Two Board members seemed to agree with the Council. Mr. Lamb and Mr. Wopschall both talked against the increase at some length; and, finally, at the suggestion of Mr. Lamb, the amount was cut to $30,000, providing for the early return of only probationary teachers. It was the first time Mr. Goslin was handed a setback, and it could be chalked up as a small but definite victory for the School Development Council.

Throughout most of the Council's stormy career—a career that, before Mr. Goslin was through, was to take a leading role in the school system's activities—a hardy band of women stood out above their fellows as being particularly active and persistent. Two of them, Mrs. Janet Schwartz and Mrs. Frances Bartlett, were wives of physicians; one, Mrs. Cay Hallberg, was the daughter of a physician; and another, Louise Hawkes Padelford, was the daughter of a rich and retired onetime New Jersey senator. Each in her own way was to contribute a great deal to the cause of Mr. Goslin's opposition. Mrs. Bartlett was avidly interested in what she thought were the subversive influences in the schools, an interest that caused her to do enormous research on such things as what textbooks were used, on who the visiting lecturers were, and on Willard Goslin's connections with national organizations. Mrs. Schwartz, although not as strong on the research, attended many Board meetings, often asked needling questions, and followed the doings of the Administration with unfailing tenacity. She also made speeches in other cities describing the evils of modern education and telling what they were doing about it in Pasadena. Mrs. Hallberg, an astute and crisp little woman who grew up in Minnnesota where her father was on the staff of the Mayo Clinic, had only one purpose—to get rid of Willard Goslin because he was a leading exponent of what she described darkly as "Modern Pragmatic Education." Nothing else mattered to her; and even after she got out of School Development Council, which she did much later, following a policy argument, she continued in her spirited campaign to get Mr. Goslin out of the school system. The last of the little band, Louise Hawkes Padelford, was, and is, in a class by herself.

Although a few local competitors might disagree—possibly for reasons approaching sheer jealousy—Louise Hawkes Padelford is without question one of the handsomest matrons in Pasadena. She is tall and lithe, impeccably dressed and beautifully poised. She is rich in grace, charm, and cold hard cash. She lives with her husband Morgan, a Technicolor executive, and two adopted children in a Spanish-type mansion perched securely in the center of several wooded acres high in the hills overlooking Pasadena. Its spacious living room affords a fine view of the city; its library is stocked with good books that give the impression of being well thumbed and well read. Mrs. Padelford has clear blue eyes that look out at the world with wide-open frankness; her ear is keen, her wit quick, and her smile enchanting. She is given to saying things with a disarming self-deprecation. She is not above "poor little me" when it seems to suit the occasion, and she sometimes runs to more memorable phrases. In a discussion she was once known to bow to the superior knowledge of a cohort by saying, "Let her tell you; she knows more about it than muddle-puddle me."

Mrs. Padelford founded, a few years back, the local chapter in Pasadena of an organization known as Pro America. Pro America originally got under way in Seattle when old Mrs. Theodore Roosevelt, stopping off in the Northwest on her way to the Philippines, became shocked at the waves of waterfront strikes then engulfing the city and proposed to a group of society women that they join together to combat them. Pro America was, in the beginning, a highly cultured garden-club species of political plant life, and still retains much of its original society glitter. Its members are mostly well-to-do, and, except for a few newcomers whom they identify as "Constitutional Democrats," they are the kind of Republicans who talk about American heritage as though it were a special privilege belonging to the privileged few. Today there are Pro America units and many members in most Pacific coast cities. Reporting Pro America activities early this year, the Los Angeles *Times*, which has always been friendly to its aims, devoted a Society Page column to a meeting of the local unit at which one George W. Robnett of Chicago gave an address. Mr. Robnett, who was identified as a director of the Church League of America and of the National Layman's Council, has long been a favorite orator at Pro America rallies. At this one his subject was what he termed the "Four Horsemen of '51." They were, he said, Stalinism, Trumanism, Welfarism, and Minorityism. His most interesting definition, as paraphrased by the *Times,* was of Minorityism: "the new national disease which is resulting in pressure groups and rousing class against class." "These four horsemen," Mr. Robnett said in conclusion, "must be bridled and tamed."

Some of Mrs. Padelford's sister members of Pro America were also members of the School Development Council. In fact, there were times during the past year when those who tried to sift out the facts were unable to tell precisely where the operations of School Development Council left off and Pro America took over, especially during the most hectic days of the anti-Goslin campaign. Certainly Pro America had the added significance of being a more widespread organization, and its spearhead, Mrs. Padelford, was a woman with many connections in the East with whom she kept in constant touch. It was small wonder that, when things were coming to a boil in Pasadena, speakers from the School Development Council were heard to quote consciously or unconsciously from the writings of persons several thousand miles from California, agreeing, apparently, with what those people said about the public-school system in the United States.

For some months following its modest efforts to cut Mr. Goslin's first budget, the School Development Council had no public activity at all. Then, in December, Willard Goslin himself was asked to speak at a Council meeting. The more impartial members of his audience have since reported that he gave an excellent talk, including a comprehensive and lucid presentation of problems confronting teachers and a lament that there wasn't more good teacher material available. He also discussed the poor balance between Federal and State taxes—the Federal Government gets a great deal in taxes compared with the State, and yet contributes nothing to the schools. In the question period that followed Mr. Goslin's talk, a woman got up and asked if he approved of the Federal Aid to Education Bill. He replied, deliberately and with force, "I approve of Federal *aid* to education, but I do not approve of Federal *control* of education." Despite the fact that a great many educators all over the country have felt and expressed this same sentiment, it was enough for this particular audience. Mrs. Padelford, an articulate opponent of Federal Aid to Education, didn't like it at all, and told Mr. Goslin as much in hardly "muddle-puddle" terms after the meeting was over. Had there been before any doubts as to where she and other members of the School Development Council stood on Willard Goslin, they were now being dispelled.

9

Mr. Goslin Faces a Money Problem

When the average citizen is interested in a school budget at all, he wants to know only three things: is the budget going up; if so, is the increase necessary; and how much more will the increase cost him personally. But when a superintendent interests himself in his budget, as he is obliged to do annually, he is faced with a number of irrefutable facts plus a number of arguable theories that could easily swing the balance between a good educational program and a poor one. In times like these, he must face such hard realities as the increased cost of building maintenance and operation and of doing business in the new buildings; the increased cost of supplies; and the increase caused by automatic raises of teachers on his payroll. He must also determine the less-easily determinable basis for raising salaries of good teachers, not only to meet the higher living costs but also to help them become better teachers. He must decide on what extra teacher-training is necessary, and what curriculum will give his students the best education. He must know what his sources of revenue are. And, being a public servant, he must obey the budget and tax laws of his State.

In the early spring of 1950, Willard Goslin, confronted with these matters, sat down with his advisers to prepare budgets for the following school year. Before him were the usual assortment of basic facts and, to boot, some special problems that could not easily be solved, especially in the elementary schools.

Pasadena's public schools have three budgets—one for the junior colleges, one for the junior high schools, and one for the elementary schools. Because the junior-college and junior-high districts cover exactly the same territory, while preparing the budget a surplus in the till of one district may be transferred to the till of the other district. This happy state of affairs, however, is not true of Pasadena's elementary-school district, which does not take in the same territory as the other two. Thus the elementary district must act, in money matters, as a separate entity, and go its own way. And, because the elementary enrollment had risen almost 50 per cent in six years, and promised to double before long, this district was Mr. Goslin's special headache in 1950.

After a great deal of round-table talk and deliberation, Mr. Goslin and his Administration arrived at the conclusion that the 1950–1951 budget should be raised by a sizable amount, and they so prepared their preliminary figures for school Board approval. The increase needed, they decided, was some $387,-000, which would raise the total elementary budget to approximately $3,860,000. The largest single item in this increase was $247,000 for additional teachers' salaries—some $40,000 of that being for automatic raises, some more for cost-of-living and merit raises, and, by far the largest item, slightly over $100,000 for eighteen new teachers and three new principals for the three new elementary schools. Another costly item was the shifting of those kindergarten classes still on a substandard

135-minute daily schedule to a 180-minute-day routine, a schedule that *all* kindergarten classes must be on, according to California law, by the 1951–1952 school year or forfeit their share of State aid.

All other costs of running the schools were up, and the Administration budgeted accordingly. Operating costs had risen from $45,000 to $54,000; maintenance costs by $30,000; undistributed reserve, an important item to any budgeteer in a day of unpredictables, had been raised by $39,000. Lastly, the Administration inserted a figure of $32,000 for what was termed "auxiliary services," which mainly meant an increase in the health service staff necessitated by the new schools, and the introduction of a new psychological service that had been recommended by one of Mr. Goslin's advisory committees.

Those were the broad outlines of the new budget, prepared in March for preliminary study and for discussion, as usual, in school Board sessions. The question then arose: Where was the money to come from to finance this increase?

Like its counterparts in other California cities and towns, Pasadena's public schools get their money from two sources. The State of California contributes a portion based on many factors, including the wealth of the community involved, and the balance comes from taxes that a school district is empowered to levy on assessed value of real estate. In the case of Pasadena, the State in 1950 was contributing about 45 per cent of the total. The other 55 per cent was coming from a tax levy whose legal maximum since 1937 had stood at $0.90 for each $100 assessed valuation.

By 1950, Pasadena property values had risen some 79 per cent since 1940, and State aid had risen in the same period. At the same time, however, enrollment was up 49 per cent and the cost of doing business was up 111 per cent. The cost of running the schools, therefore, had more than kept pace with an increased income. As Willard Goslin got his 1950–1951 budget ready for inspection, he was confronted with the blunt fact that in order to spend more money on Pasadena's schools, the tax limit would have to be raised. And, of course, the only way to raise the tax limit was to have an election. The people of the city must decide.

Having discussed with the Board the need for a raise in the tax limit—and hence the need for an election—the next decision was how much more to ask for. To satisfy the new budget, approximately $0.30 per $100 assessment additional was needed. But Mr. Goslin was taking the long view. Even though the electorate might vote permission to raise a tax-levy limit, that did not mean that the Board would spend up to the limit the very first year, or even at any time in the near future. After all, the $0.90 limit had only been levied and used for three years of the thirteen it was in existence. And so Mr. Goslin proposed to the Board that they go before the people the following June and ask for a tax levy limit of $1.35—an increase of $0.45, or 50 per cent over the old ceiling of $0.90. This would, he said, take care of the increased needs for the next five years. The Board promptly saw Mr. Goslin's point, and on April 12 it voted unanimously to call an election to vote on the new limit. The election was set for June 2.

Up to that moment, Mr. Goslin knew hardly anything about the School Development Council, and nothing at all about Frank William Wells, who had just been elected its president. But from a day in April when Mr. Wells appeared before the

Board of Education to discuss the forthcoming election until the night of June 2, Mr. Goslin and the rest of Pasadena were to hear a great deal from the Council and from Mr. Wells. A battle was about to be joined; and, as it turned out, it was to be a fight to the finish.

10

Mr. Wells and the Tax Election

Frank Wells got into the School Development Council, it seems, almost by accident. As a resident of Pasadena for only four years, and as the head of his own small company producing digging equipment, he was minding his business in the winter of 1949–1950 when a sequence of events suddenly thrust him into the driver's seat.

By that winter the School Development Council had reached a low ebb. Meetings were few, membership had dropped off, and new blood was badly needed. The blood was obtained in most enterprising fashion. Pasadena's tabloid *Independent*—a newspaper which had seldom been friendly to the school system even in John Sexson's day—had recently invited its readers to write in and tell the newspaper what they thought was wrong with Pasadena's schools. The invitation was greeted warmly by dissatisfied parents. Quite a few letters came in, and the *Independent* printed them. And when Mr. Ebersole asked if he could have a list of the dissatisfied parents and their home addresses, the *Independent*'s management obliged. The SDC then sent postcards and made telephone calls to the *Independ-*

ent's friends asking them to a meeting to discuss the latest ills of the Pasadena system.

Up to this time Frank Wells himself had not paid much attention to the SDC, but his wife, a former Iowa schoolteacher and now the mother of two children in Pasadena's schools, had gone to meetings more or less regularly ever since it was founded. And now, when the clarion call went out, Mrs. Wells persuaded her husband to go along to the meeting. Once more about a hundred people showed up. This time they were divided into groups—parents of elementary-school children in one, parents of high schoolers in another, parents of junior-college students in a third. One of the groups was assigned to the lively Ruth Wells, whose husband joined her. Mr. Wells now remembers that everybody talked at once, and that "everybody had criticisms of the schools. . . . So I said if that's the way you all feel, something ought to be done about it."

Once more a committee was formed; once more it went off and pondered for a week or so; and once more, in the Legion Hall, it reported back its recommendations. At that meeting the executive committee elected Frank Wells its chairman. "I accepted it," he says, "but I made the point that many people would have to share the work load, as this was an avocation with me." The SDC's old friend, Mrs. Frances Bartlett, was again put on that committee, along with Cay Hallberg and the Messrs. Ebersole, Petterson, and an insurance man named E. Felton Taylor. It was, in effect, old home week in the Council.

One of the first things Mr. Wells and his associates did was to invite a couple of school Board members to lunch, to "reach out," as he said, "the hand of friendship." Mr. Lamb and Mr. Wopschall went willingly enough because, as Mr. Wopschall later said, they thought these were simply citizens interested in promoting the welfare of the schools, who "wanted to do something constructive." Mr. Wells was pleased with the co-operation extended him by the two gentlemen, although apparently it was never made clear that he was acting in the capacity of Chairman of the SDC. This equable get-together notwithstanding, however, it was not long before Frank Wells and the school Board were to be locked in bitter combat.

On April 12 Mr. Wells went to his first meeting of the Board of Education. He knew what was up. That day, as he sat quietly listening, the tax election was proposed, voted upon, and unanimously passed. As Mr. Wells so vividly described the scene: "Wham!—the proposal went right through, in a couple of minutes. There was no first and second reading." Not at that time being very familiar with Board procedure, Mr. Wells was naturally unaware that on matters of this sort the Board did not need to plod through "first and second readings." The preliminary outlines of the budget had been duly discussed in Board sessions, and the Board and the Administration had jointly told the public about them at a demonstration in the McKinley Junior High School. It had been evident to the Board that, to raise funds to carry on the system's present program, an election had to be held. The public could not be expected to vote on *whether* an election would be held; it would have its say at the election itself.

It had now become apparent to Mr. Wells and his friends that no time was to be lost if the voice of the School Development Council was to be heard. And so it was that, at the next meeting of the Board—on April 19—Mr. Wells got up and made the first of a provocative series of speeches. Before he did so, however, a most significant and closely related side issue—the business of rezoning boundary lines for junior high schools—was aired at the meeting.

As most Pasadenans knew by this time, two new junior high schools, Temple City and La Cañada, would soon be opened. And today, as had been announced, rezoning to take care of the two new schools would be discussed. The place was packed. The first speaker on the subject was Willard Goslin himself.

Mr. Goslin opened by explaining that it was the Administration's duty "from time to time" to set up new attendance boundaries so that students would be sent to the most convenient schools. In the present instance, Mr. Goslin said, the opening of the two new schools and a general growth in population would require the readjustment of practically all boundary lines, affecting all five of the existing schools plus the two to be opened. Then he proceeded to describe in some detail the factors involved in setting up lines—the number of students in the areas, the facilities available at each place, the distance involved between homes and schools, problems of transportation and hazards of traffic. Recommendations for rezoning, Mr. Goslin told his audience, along with details of the problems and a map indicating locations, were available for each person to take home and read. "In order to meet the responsibility to groups of citizens who had asked time to study the Administration's proposal," Mr. Goslin said, the presentation today was informal. Two weeks later the formal recommendation would be presented for Board approval.

One of the strongest rezoning dissenters to speak that day was a man named John R. Holmes, president of the East Arroyo Association, an organization of local property owners who had banded together to guard their real-estate interests against any encroachments or danger signs. Mr. Holmes made his position, and that of his Association, perfectly clear. They wished to register the strongest kind of objection to sending their teen-agers to Washington Junior High School, even though it was much nearer home, instead of to La Cañada, which, although it was across the Arroyo, had a privileged class of pupils. And they also wished to register the strongest kind of objection to any future rezoning that would send their younger children to an elementary school that did not have a top-drawer clientele instead of to the Linda Vista School, also across the dry river, where by common consent privileged children had always gone. The East Arroyo Association's various speakers that day made no bones about the fact that rezoning would reduce some of their property values. What they did not say in so many words, but what was perfectly plain, was that they were afraid those property values would decline because children in the affected neighborhoods would have to attend classes with Negro and Mexican children.

After this opposition had had its say, the matter of rezoning was then put off, to be voted on two weeks hence. Next on the agenda was Mr. Frank William Wells.

Up to this moment Pasadena in general, and the school Board in particular, knew so little about Frank Wells that in the minutes of this meeting he was described as an attorney, and he was again called an attorney the next day in the *Star-News,* although he had never studied law.

The man the crowd in the conference room saw that day was a short, trim individual with a flashing smile. The voice they heard was something like Harry Truman's, Midwestern and slightly nasal and very twangy, the kind of voice that delighted some listeners and irritated others, depending mainly on whether the listeners agreed or disagreed with what Mr. Wells had to say.

What Frank Wells had to say that day was plain enough. He had before him a petition which he said was signed by some eight hundred people (it was later established as a matter of record that the signatures numbered fewer than fifty), asking that the Board postpone the June 2 tax election so that his group, the Pasadena School Development Council, would have the "necessary time" to study and evaluate the need for an increase in the tax rate. Then, stumbling over some words—a homely mannerism that was to endear him to a number of followers in the days to come—he explained how "we as citizens" (presumably meaning members of the SDC) had been "promised" last fall that "we should have copies of the proposed budget in detail several months in advance—so as to have ample time for study and consideration. This promise has not been kept. Even at this late date no such budget has been presented and the superintendent of schools now states that it cannot be ready before May."

"We desire as taxpayers and parents," Mr. Wells said in his wind-up, "to be helpful and constructive, but until we have the necessary financial information and time to study it we cannot properly judge the needs."

Mr. Wells's petition was mystifying to the Board and to the Administration on several counts. For one thing, no one had heard anything about the School Development Council for some little time, and many now wondered how it had suddenly come to be a self-appointed and major spokesman for citizens and parents. But that was minor: any group, large or small, significant or insignificant, could have its day before the Board. Of more moment was this business of "Board members" having "promised" the SDC anything. Mr. Wopschall might possibly recall that informal lunch with the Messrs. Ebersole and Petterson some months before; and he could certainly recall that more recent lunch at which Mr. Wells also was on hand. But Mr. Wopschall knew that no member of the Board, as an individual, could have "promised" any group anything: commitments could only be made by the Board in meetings officially assembled. No one was more surprised, Mr. Wopschall said later, than he to be confronted now by Frank Wells as chairman of the School Development Council, urging that the election be postponed.

As for the budget itself, it was quite true that a complete breakdown had not yet been prepared; but as most people by this time knew, its general outlines had been previously aired, most publicly, at the McKinley Junior High meeting, complete with charts and figures. That had taken place on March 29—two weeks before the present meeting. And, although Mr. Wells had not been there, members of the Parent-Teachers Association Council—a body that also represented fathers and mothers of school children—had. Moreover, these members had reported back to the PTA Council itself, which, on April 10, had by unanimous vote agreed to support the new budget. It therefore seemed rather odd to many people that Mr. Wells, representing the School Development Council, appeared so lacking in knowledge of what had gone on.

After Mr. Wells had made his earnest plea, Mr. Goslin got up to reply. He had never had the pleasure of seeing Frank Wells before, and so far as Mr. Goslin knew, Mr. Wells had never attempted, in his new capacity as SDC chairman, to get in touch with him. Today, however, Mr. Goslin was courteous and patient as he replied to Mr. Wells. He explained that the procedures for setting up the budget were orderly and followed the rules laid down by the Education Code. He outlined the steps the Administration was following in keeping the community informed so far as was possible. And he said that the Board was fully up to date on all budget planning.

Next to speak was Milton Wopschall, who was now president of the Board. Once again he tried to make it clear that the request for an additional $0.45 tax levy did not mean the entire sum would be levied the first year, or, probably, any year soon. He suggested to Mr. Wells that he and his SDC sit down with Business Director Marsee and explore the budget in detail. He stated that all figures would be available to Mr. Wells, and that he, Wopschall, "felt certain" that the School Development Council would then agree that the tax-rate increase was justified.

In reply Frank Wells said: "We aren't protesting that the tax rate increase is unnecessary. . . . What we are saying is that we have not been given the necessary information required to properly judge the needs. Even if we do meet with Dr. Marsee, we'll have little time to study over the facts. June 2 is not very far away. . . ."

Thereupon several other members of the audience, echoing Mr. Wells's petition, claimed they didn't have enough advance information on the budget, and Mr. Wopschall again replied. The election, he explained, had to be held in June for two reasons—so that the final budget could be prepared by August, when by law it had to be ready, and so that the schools could be opened on time in September. Before the meeting was over, many other people had many other things to say. Finally, Attorney Brydolf, also with infinite patience, assured the gathering that there would be ample notice given the community on budget schedules and on announcements of meeting between then and election day. He also assured them that it was the Board's earnest desire to keep the citizens of Pasadena informed of its monetary needs. Thereupon the Board voted, unanimously, to go through with the election on schedule, on June 2.

Four days after this Board meeting, Frank Wells let his cat out of the bag, and it was to romp helter-skelter from that day forward through the night of June 1. On April 24 the School Development Council held a rousing meeting at American Legion Hall, which had been such a favorite camping ground during the Council's spasmodic life, and there Frank Wells read to his followers a lengthy statement of great significance. It was plain to everyone that here, at last, was the School Development Council's declaration of policy. As such, it sharply deviated from what Mr. Wells had said in his petition read before the Board only four days before.

"The Council," Mr. Wells read, "believes in adequate school facilities and in high-quality, well-paid teachers and proposes to analyze the school budget and expenditures with the idea of getting better results from every tax dollar. During this time it believes that additional costs due to new teaching innovations should not be entertained except to accomplish demonstrable benefits. . . .

"The best judges of the success of our educational system are those who employ and work with its products. Those best qualified to know what is taking place in the system are parents of the children who are undergoing the process. This evaluation is far superior to the theories of those administering the process, or of abstract written tests of somewhat questionable validity.

"While we have supported education with our dollars, we

have neglected to guide it with our principles. This we propose to remedy by more diligent investigation and concerted action when such is necessary in order to prevent further deterioration."

After this preamble, Mr. Wells got down to the heart of the matter. He minced no words.

"We are alarmed," he continued, "and deeply concerned over the program of education as it is being developed in this community. We feel that definite steps must be taken to develop a program of teaching and learning that will produce boys and girls who are better prepared to function adequately in all they do. This involves a more thorough mastery of the fundamental tools in addition to the ways in which they will be used.

"We believe the best way of attaining this is in classes where the basic subjects, taught thoroughly and individually, make up the bulk of the activity. . . . When we mention subjects we refer to English, reading, spelling, penmanship, geography, civics, historical background of American life, and the sciences.

"We believe that grades are the best measure of a pupil's achievement and should be maintained in as objective a manner as possible. . . . We further believe that if teachers could be relieved from so many 'meetings' to devote time to their actual class work or to relaxation, that better results would be obtained in the classroom learning situation. . . . We believe [in] self control and courteous behavior [for] every boy and girl . . . better discipline . . . proper work habits. . . . We believe that our American heritage should be made a part of every student's understanding, and that a deep appreciation of his rights and duties as an American citizen be instilled within. . . .

"We believe that education in Pasadena needs not only our dollars, but our principles and our personal time and interest, and this we propose to provide through this organized group."

The best evidence that Mr. Wells's group was organized came at once, when a vote was taken on his statement. It was adopted unanimously. Then the meeting got on to the matter of discussing the tax election. And on this subject John Petterson had something to say: "We may be in favor of the tax limit increase . . . but we do not believe in handing out a blank check. . . . The Administration says that it will not require the full 45 cent increase, which would return $675,000 in the first year, but would need only $300,000. I don't like to hand someone my pocketbook and say, 'I know you only want a dollar but here's what I have; use what you want. . . .' We want to know what we're paying for."

Thus, at last and in public—the *Star-News* gave it over two columns the next day—the Pasadena School Development Council had with clarity and without equivocation come forth with its real objectives: "to prevent further deterioration" in the Pasadena school system, and to change that system radically and fundamentally. No one could question the basic soundness of any statement of principles that had for its aim educating children properly and thoroughly. But whether the School Development Council was the proper authority to judge the merits of an existing system, and, by the same set of rules, whether that system was so incalculably poor, were subjects widely open to question. And whether these matters should be injected into, and hopelessly confused with, a forthcoming election for a tax-levy increase was certainly something else that could be debated with authority and reason.

On April 26 the school Board held its next regular meeting.

At this session Mr. Goslin was ready with a more detailed analysis of the budget—an analysis which, he said, was usually not ready until June, but which was being presented early for public inspection this year because of the impending election. Answering a question asked by Milton Wopschall, Mr. Goslin explained that this presentation was simply an elaboration of the budget outlined three weeks before at McKinley Junior High, including all the details asked for.

Frank Wells was again present. If he was at all interested in these details, or was grateful to have them, he did not say so. Instead, he asked once more for postponement of the June 2 election—this time, he explained, until a committee could be formed to study the budget requirements. This committee, as he outlined it, should consist of "one member of the Real Estate Board, one from the taxpayers' committee of the Chamber of Commerce, one from the Pasadena School Development Council, and a consulting expert on school board budgets."

The pro-Administration reaction to his proposal was best expressed by a woman who now rose to challenge Mr. Wells. His suggestion, she said, cast a serious reflection on the Board and on the Administration. "As a parent and a taxpayer," she had "great confidence" in Mr. Goslin and in his Administration. Moreover she wanted to know why, if the Board were considering forming any such committee, representatives of a number of other groups should not be included to make it a true cross section of Pasadena—groups such as PTA, the Women's Civic League, the League of Women Voters, and the like. Had not these organizations also a real stake in the city and in its school system?

After the chairman of a Committee of the Pasadena Council of Churches had endorsed this sentiment, Mr. Wopschall observed that "all groups" have a right to study the budget, and that the Board would be happy indeed to receive suggestions from any of them. Mr. Wells had no more comment to make—then.

Five days later, without waiting for the Board to take action on his latest proposal, the School Development Council, in conjunction with the Property Owners Division of the Realty Board and the Chamber of Commerce, announced they planned to make their own investigation. It was to be conducted by a Los Angeles tax analyst named Louis J. Kroeger, who would look into the Elementary School Budget, and report back to them before the election. As everyone remembered only too well, on April 19 Mr. Wells had asked that the election be postponed because the date gave too little time to study the need for a tax levy. Now, three weeks later, with the election still set for June 2, the time had been found.

Mr. Kroeger and his associates went to work for the Council, the Chamber of Commerce, and the Property Owners Division, and for a few days the Development Council itself remained relatively quiet. Frank Wells had not yet started on his series of radio talks and public forums. Mr. Goslin and the Board, not yet aware of the lengths to which the opposition intended to go, began to prepare for the election in more or less routine fashion, with little planned publicity and little attention to the opposition.

In the meantime the delicate and troublesome subject of rezoning the junior high schools had come before the Board for discussion and final action. It, too, was to have a bearing on the June 2 election.

On May 3, as promised, the Board sat in conclave to listen to what interested groups had to say on rezoning. There were few surprises. John R. Holmes was present, again representing the East Arroyo Association; and once more he requested that children in his area be permitted to go to school in the area west of the Arroyo. He again made his plea that the same thing be done for the Linda Vista Elementary School. The president of the Pasadena Realty Board, John S. Moore, read a letter from his Board stating that "the proposed change in zoning will have a definite effect on property values," and asked the Board of Education to look further into the problem before coming to a final decision. Other people representing other to-be-affected communities read similar letters and petitions. The most vocal and the frankest of these was a statement by one Wellslake D. Morse, who said flatly that to him it looked as though the Administration was making this thing a racial issue, and nothing else. Would the Board please clarify?

Mr. Wopschall asked Mr. Goslin to do so, and, once more, Mr. Goslin did. This was not, he explained, a racial issue or any other single issue. You have so many school facilities, and they are located in this and that territory; you have so many children living in well defined areas; distances between homes and schools must be taken into account; and so must natural boundaries and hazards. He said once again that the Administration "has no interest in who lives on which side of the boundaries." Its interest was to put the right number of children in the proper facilities in the most logical and workable manner possible.

At this point a number of men and women, representing many different kinds of Pasadena organizations, including college groups, women's leagues, church organizations, and councils on education, spoke up on behalf of the rezoning plan as outlined by Mr. Goslin.

Mr. Wopschall looked around the room to make sure everyone had had his say, to make sure no one was being shortchanged. Then he announced that, in line with what Mr. Goslin had said, the Board saw no reason why the new boundaries should not be set according to the needs of the school system and the community as a whole. Whereupon he called for a vote. By unanimous consent, the Board of Education then set the new boundaries for the schools. The matter had been settled to Mr. Goslin's complete satisfaction. But he was not to hear the end of it. Some property owners were not to let him forget in a hurry what they thought he had done to them. Neither were some parents who did not like the prospect of their children mingling in school with nonwhites.

On the tax front, events were moving right along. Louis Kroeger began his analysis of the Pasadena schools on May 3, when Mr. Wells brought him to the Board of Education offices for quick interviews with two members of the Board, Mr. Wopschall and Mr. Brydolf. Then he was taken in to meet Mr. Goslin and Dr. Marsee. He saw Dr. Gilchrist for about fifteen minutes in Dr. Marsee's office. Nine days later Mr. Kroeger came forth with what he officially called a "Budgetary Analysis of the Pasadena City (Elementary) School District." It was a strange and contradictory document, and when Mr. Goslin and his associates read it, they lost no time in saying so.

The report's first sentence itself was frank and open. "This is a brief report," it said, "of the results of a brief study. . . . What conclusions will be drawn from these facts—and what action will be taken—remains the responsibility of each organization. Because of limited time available for the study, this report does not pretend to be based on a detailed analysis of certain basic facts. . . ."

What basic facts were set forth by the report seemed sound enough—the "substantial increase" of the elementary budget since 1940; the "steady increase in enrollment" in the same period; the average assessed valuation per pupil as compared to other districts in the county (of the list of nine, Pasadena was, surprisingly, fourth from last); the average cost per pupil (here Pasadena was third, outranked only by two other rich communities, Beverly Hills and Santa Monica), and a number of related and indisputable items.

The "basic facts" out of the way, the report next outlined "the problem"—whether the voters should approve a rate increase, and its two "related questions": "Is the proposed budget sound?" and, "Is the educational program satisfactory?" Then, having granted that "the effectiveness and acceptability of the educational program cannot be measured by a quick study," it said that, "If the program can be supported within the present tax limit—and if there are ways to keep it within the limit for several years ahead—the voters ought to veto the proposed increase." But, on the other hand, "If the existing program requires even a few cents of increase over the existing limit—and if the voters want at least the present program continued—then the sound thing to do is to approve the increase."

Having posed the pros and cons in a manner that surely could not have offended anyone, and at the same time was not particularly enlightening to anyone, Mr. Kroeger then proceeded to take his clients step by step through the budget as it was currently set up. As he went along he pointed out where big and little savings might be effected. Employing such phrases as "Some reduction in budget could safely be made if," "We see the possibility of saving," "There can be a saving if," "We believe it possible to reduce," Mr. Kroeger, unconsciously or otherwise, managed to convey to his clients precisely what his clients wanted to hear. He came forward with some interesting suggestions: that when new teachers are hired to replace those who died or left the system, they be hired at minimum rates; that some "additional personnel" be eliminated; that maintenance staffs for new schools be employed "only nine months" and "at lower salaries than estimated"; that "proposed increases" for upkeep of grounds, repair of buildings, replacement of equipment, and additions of buildings be sliced by 50 per cent. Last of all, he suggested that the "undistributed reserve" be cut by $35,000.

In his "Conclusions," Mr. Kroeger came right out with it: "In our judgment," he reported, "the proposed budget can be reduced to the extent discussed above and summarized below." That summary listed ten items totaling a saving of $225,407. This was quite a saving, Mr. Goslin and his associates thought, for a survey that had started out by describing its mission as fact-finding and necessarily "brief"—for a survey which promised that "conclusions" would remain the "responsibility of" the three organizations retaining him to make the study. Mr. Goslin would reasonably be expected to wonder when a fact was a fact, and when a conclusion was a conclusion.

On May 16, four days after Mr. Goslin and his staff had been presented with the Kroeger report, the Administration came out with a sharp and critical reply, opening up with a blast objecting to the brief amount of time Mr. Kroeger had spent at 351 South Hudson Avenue. "In the preparation of his report," Mr. Goslin wrote, "Mr. Kroeger spent not to exceed seven hours with Dr. Marsee and his associates in the Business

Division of the school system. Dr. Robert S. Gilchrist, Assistant Superintendent of Schools in charge of Instruction, was called in for a brief period of about fifteen minutes during one of the conferences in Marsee's office. . . . He did not discuss educational needs with Dr. Gilchrist. At no time did Mr. Kroeger seek a conference with the Superintendent of Schools. There are no indications that he held conferences with principals, supervisors, or teachers who might have been able to reflect the needs of the Elementary Schools. . . . [In his introduction] Mr. Kroeger [said] 'This report does not pretend to be based on a detailed analysis. . . .' We want to ask, 'On what basis would a valid report be based EXCEPT on a detailed analysis of the *organization, operations* and *program* of a school system?' "

The Goslin response also went item by item through Mr. Kroeger's fact-findings. Mr. Goslin found in them what he considered serious errors, omissions, and inconsistencies. His answer was thorough and, to many of its readers, it answered reasonably and convincingly the Kroeger proposals for reductions.

On May 21 Mr. Kroeger replied in kind. He stuck by his guns and, in his turn, took up Mr. Goslin's answers item by item. "We have seen press reports of comments in reply by the Superintendent of Schools. Some of them have to do with the merits of the case, and some are merely uncomplimentary generalities about our work. It is an old trick, when facts and reasoning are weak, to resort to abuse. . . ."

By the time the exchange of brickbats had found its way into print, much damage had been done to prospects for a favorable tax election. After the Kroeger report was first released to the press, on May 14, the Pasadena papers flatly called it a recommendation to reduce the budget. The *Star-News* headlined its story: REPORT TELLS HOW TO CUT $225,407 FROM SCHOOL BUDGET, RETAIN PROGRAM. That same day the *Star-News* also carried a story announcing that the School Development Council was recommending a No vote on June 2 because "The Kroeger report proves that the Pasadena Elementary School District budget can be safely cut so that no increase in the tax rate will be necessary." The word "proves" was enlightening.

11

The People Go to the Polls

While Frank Wells and his followers went on damning the Board of Education, the budget, the Goslin Administration, the Pasadena schools, and Progressive Education, a number of individuals and civic groups made a belated effort to come to the defense of the tax. Douglas G. Woolf, editor and publisher of a weekly called the *East Pasadena Herald,* valiantly and continuously supported the Goslin Administration and the tax elections. Overriding its taxpayers' committee, the Chamber of Commerce voted in favor of it. So did a number of other organizations around town. And William L. Blair, who had been on the Board for so many years, pulled together a Citizens Committee for School Tax Support which held several organizational meetings, compiled figures showing the need for the new levy, ran several "Vote Yes" advertisements, and held a mass meeting at which *both* sides were asked to air their views.

The net result of all this earnest endeavor was small and ineffectual. After they had once come out in favor of the tax, many groups seemed to feel their duty had been done, and did nothing more. Hardly a speech was made for the Goslin side that found its way into the newspapers. And the very fact that

Mr. Blair's committee had politely invited the opposition to speak at its rally seemed to indicate that those supporting the tax failed to measure, by a wide margin, the strength and power of that opposition. The voices of these well meaning people were feeble and timid compared with the clamorings of Frank Wells and the realty interests. At the meetings of the SDC, people whose views differed from theirs were not allowed a hearing.

By the time Frank Wells opened up the last ten days of his barrage with a mammoth mass meeting on May 22 at Madison Elementary School, the School Development Council had acquired some fresh ammunition. It came from a most unexpected quarter. How it found its way to Pasadena is something of a mystery, but the fact that it did was to have reverberations not only in Pasadena, but all over the country.

Until he mentioned them, it is quite doubtful if many of Frank Wells's listeners in the Madison School had ever heard of Allen Alderson Zoll or an organization with the impressive name of the National Council for American Education. It is doubtful, too, if many other Pasadena citizens had ever heard of Mr. Zoll and the NCAE, until, eventually—when it was too late—some of them took the trouble to look the man up.

Back in the days when the rabble-rousing Father Coughlin was raving and ranting every week on the radio, vilifying Franklin Roosevelt, the New Deal, and the Jews and praising the Christian Front, Allen Zoll was one of his staunchest supporters and admirers. Mr. Zoll has also, at one time or another, been working friend with such anti-Semitic gentlemen as Gerald H. K. Smith and Merwin Hart. The Attorney General once dubbed one of his now defunct organizations "Fascist and subversive." Once Zoll was indicted for allegedly attempting to extort money from New York's radio station WMCA. Although he pleaded not guilty and the indictment was later nol-prossed, the publicity was pretty gamey and, for a time following its quashing, Mr. Zoll wasn't heard from. Then, in 1948, he opened up a suite of offices in New York City and announced the founding of the National Council for American Education. This must not be confused with the reputable National Education Association or the equally reputable American Council on Education. Mr. Zoll's outfit was formed for the ostensible purpose of eradicating "Socialism, Communism and all forms of Marxism from the schools and colleges of America, and to stimulate sound American education."

Toward that end Mr. Zoll, who describes himself as an "internationally known sales consultant," began to publish from time to time a series of pamphlets with such provocative titles as "*Red*ucators at Harvard," "Should Americans Be Against World Government," "They WANT Your Child," and "Progressive Education *Increases* Delinquency." Each was for sale at $0.20 for single copies (with stamps acceptable), six copies for $1.00, fifty copies for $5.00, 1,000 copies for $60, and a "special price for larger quantities." Membership in the NCAE cost anywhere from $5 for the associate type to $1,000 and up, at which point the contributor was entitled to be called "Benefactor." As a further contribution to his cause, Mr. Zoll began to publish a monthly bulletin called *Educational Guardian,* the price of which ranged from gratis for one copy to $35 for 1,000.

When he started out in 1948, Mr. Zoll wrote to a number of important people and asked them to sponsor the new National Council for American Education. As busy people are so likely to do, several men, including General Jonathan Wainwright, Stanley High of *Reader's Digest,* Senator Arthur Vandenberg, and Gene Tunney, agreed without finding out who Zoll was or what the NCAE was all about. Not until the New York *World-Telegram*'s Frederick Woltman wrote something of Allen Zoll's past did the Messrs. Wainwright, High, Tunney, and Vandenberg beat a hasty and embarrassed retreat from the organization. The NCAE now lists as its officers and board of governors a conglomerate assortment—a retired small-college president, a retired admiral, and several past presidents of such organizations as the Colonial Daughters of the Seventeenth Century, the United States Daughters of 1812, the Daughters of the American Revolution, the Society for Constitutional Security, and the Federation of Huguenot Societies.

Today Allen Zoll operates his NCAE from modest quarters in an old-fashioned office building at No. 1 Maiden Lane, at the corner of Broadway. All he needs to carry on the work of his NCAE is an outer office for two typists and a secretary, and two small inner offices, one for the large, portly person of Allen Zoll himself, the other mainly for stacks of old newspapers. The outer office is adorned with an American flag, a painting of the signing of the Declaration of Independence, and a number of reproductions of early American history, including a portrait of George Washington and a picture of Betsy Ross at work on the flag. Just how many members of the NCAE there are, Mr. Zoll has presistently refused to say. Nor will he, no matter how much he is pressed, give out the names of any members aside from those listed as vice presidents and on the Board. "I wouldn't even tell a congressional committee that," he has been known to declare.

There are numerous and contradictory versions of how Allen Zoll came to be mentioned by Frank Wells in Pasadena on the night of May 22, and of how one piece of his literature—"Progressive Education *Increases* Juvenile Delinquency"—got into Mr. Wells's hands for comment and praise that night—and for wide distribution. Memories are short on the subject. Louise Padelford, who was there and posed for pictures but didn't speak, believes that "one of the members" brought a copy to an earlier meeting. Mr. Wells himself is even less clear. During one interview early this year, he said (1) he may have written Mr. Zoll and asked him for some copies, then after further rumination said (2) No, he didn't write him; and then, after still more cogitation, (3) he admitted he might have done so. In New York, Mr. Zoll has refused to commit himself.

Many things Frank Wells said at the Madison School, and repeated later, paraphrased with remarkable fidelity the writings of Allen Zoll.

"So-called progressive education," Mr. Zoll wrote in the juvenile-delinquency pamphlet, "shot through as it is with the blight of Pragmatism, has had a very deleterious effect upon the original character of American education. The new movement encourages students to 'think' without the labor of learning the facts necessary to accurate thinking." "Pragmatic progressive education," Mr. Wells said in Pasadena, "has curtailed thinking by encouraging students to think without the labor of learning the facts necessary to accurate thinking."

"Those who have read the Uniform Crime Reports issued by the Department of Justice," wrote Mr. Zoll, "or even scan the headlines in the daily press, know what moral disintegration is taking place in our society. . . . The Uniform Crime Report for 1949 . . . reported that youths under 21 constituted 27.4 of those charged with major crimes. There is no possible doubt that most of this condition is directly traceable to the fatal lack of the right kind of instruction in our schools." "The Department of Justice issued a statement," said Mr. Wells in Pasadena, apparently confusing the Department with Allen Zoll, "that there is no possible doubt that most of this condition is directly traceable to the fatal lack of the right kind of instruction and discipline in our schools."

Mr. Wells had a great deal more to say that night—against the budget, against the Administration, and, most particularly, against Progressive Education. The full import of all he said and how he came to say it was a long time in getting wide distribution in Pasadena. The Sunday following the Madison School meeting, one of Pasadena's finest clergymen, Dr. Max Merritt Morrison of the Westminster Presbyterian Church, stood in his pulpit and denounced the course that meeting had taken. Had what he said been printed then, things might have been different. But it was not until three weeks later—over two weeks after the tax election—that a group of Pasadena and Altadena citizens, at last aroused, paid to have Dr. Morrison's remarks, by then extended with further facts, published as a full-page advertisement in the local papers. They still made interesting, if outdated, reading.

"I would like to call your attention," Dr. Morrison wrote, "to a disturbing element that has made its appearance in our community. . . . So evil is it that it can result in permanent injury to our community life, if we are not alert to its threatening danger. . . .

"Mrs. Morrison and I, desiring to learn as much as possible about the issues involved in the proposed tax increase—so that we might vote intelligently—decided to attend some of the various meetings. . . . We started out seeking information. . . .

"The first meeting we attended was in the Madison Elementary School, Monday evening, May 22. It was sponsored by a group called the School Development Council. It was one of the most disturbing experiences we have had since we came to Pasadena eight years ago. . . . At this meeting we heard good American citizens—men and women of Pasadena whom we have learned to admire for their service to our community—ridiculed, accused of giving sympathy to un-American activities, and our free public school education referred to as 'rubbish.' . . . Listening in on the various speakers and the un-American conduct of their sympathizers, one wanted to say what Ralph Waldo Emerson was alleged to have said at a similar meeting in his day: 'Gentlemen, please excuse me for leaving, but I must have got into the wrong meeting. I thought I was in the United States of America.' "

Dr. Morrison went on to tell how, a few days after the meeting, he set out to "get as much information" as he could about Zoll and the National Council for American Education. And then, with the thoroughness of the scholar, Dr. Morrison proceeded to itemize everything that Zoll had been up to through the years.

It was an illuminating and telling statement. But its impact on the election was, of course, nil. Indeed, up to the very day of the election no one had attempted to throw any light on the murky history of the School Development Council, or its connection, if any, with Allen Zoll whom Frank Wells quoted so assiduously.

Two days after the Madison School rally, Willard Goslin again answered the charges that were being thrown at him and the school system. At a regular meeting of the school Board, held as usual in the conference room, he did something he rarely did at Board meetings: he made a long speech.

"I would like," he said, "to make a few remarks on the attack which I think is being made on public education in this community. In doing so I would like to try once more to see if we can't get the real merits and the purpose of this election into the foreground.

"I am concerned . . . and would like again to call the community's attention to the basic facts which necessitate an increase in the elementary tax rate."

First, Mr. Goslin gave the score: enrollment up from 7,800 to 10,780 in the last five years, and an expectancy of 16,000 children by 1954; a rise in operating costs since 1937, when the $0.90 levy was put in, of 111 per cent. "There isn't any way for this town to talk its way out of the situation or to dodge it," he warned, and stated flatly, "We either raise the limit . . . or we educate our children less well."

Next he explained that the tax increase was necessary "to continue the kind of educational program which Pasadena, over a period of many years, has demonstrated it wanted, and to make a few improvements in areas which have emerged after months of study as needing improvement." Then he told of the need to equip and staff three new schools—"because we feel that every child in the community is entitled to a full day of school and because we believe that children should have the opportunity of being in classes which are not overcrowded." More money was also necessary, he said, "to help improve our salary schedule . . . to attract to Pasadena well-trained teachers. . . . It just doesn't make sense to go around town and talk about employing teachers at the minimum figure when that figure is already outmatched by many surrounding communities." Then, finally, he asked for the increase "to begin to decrease the backlog of maintenance demands which have grown up during the depression and the war. . . . We have in this office a steady barrage of complaints from PTA and other groups because our buildings haven't been maintained as they should. . . . The only way to bring our buildings up to standard is to spend more money on them."

Having had his say on the needs for an increase, Willard Goslin got down to some hard facts and strong criticism.

"I have been teaching school in America for over thirty years . . . Superintendent of Schools for twenty-five. . . . I have been mixed up in a lot of battles. There have always been some people in this country who have been opposed to public education and a few of them seem to be in Pasadena. . . . When an attack on the tax levy, that is designed specifically for the education of our own children in this community, drifts off so that attempts are made to split, weaken and divide the Board of Education, when efforts are made to discredit and destroy confidence in the ability of my hard-working and able associates; when the attacks go so far as to be dangerously close to accusing teachers of this community of being subversive, as was done on the platform of the Madison School on Monday night; and finally when the attacks get around to the kind of education program that our children need and that has been supported in this community for a long period of time; then it seems to me that the people of this community ought to know where I, as Superintendent of Schools, stand.

"All of these attacks have been a smoke screen. The point has long passed where we are debating honest differences of how much money we will spend for education. . . . The doors of the Superintendent's office and those of my associates are open, as they have continuously been, to citizens or groups of citizens who wish answers to honest questions. I will not recede one inch in the face of the kind of criticism which has been leveled against the public schools during the past several weeks and especially that criticism which came off the platform of Madison School Monday night. In addition, I want to identify my appreciation for the splendid way in which the Board of Education has interpreted the need for this tax levy. . . . I want the community to know where I stand."

Although he was to have a few more things to say, on the air and at meetings, before June 2, this was Mr. Goslin's main proclamation of policy, and as such it was duly reported in full in both Pasadena papers. In any ordinary campaign, where real issues were not clouded by the sort of propaganda the School Development Council was pouring forth, Mr. Goslin's speech surely would have struck home to many a thinking citizen. But this was not an ordinary campaign, and Mr. Goslin's adversaries were untiring in their efforts to minimize his views and render them suspect.

As June 2 drew close, Frank Wells stepped up his speaking engagements to a nightly basis, although he avoided having meetings on Sundays or Decoration Day. By now he had hit upon a few phrases that seemed to strike such a responsive chord in his audiences that he repeated them over and over again. One of his favorites was "Progressive Education Means Progressive Taxation." Another, which so impressed the Property Owners Division of the Realty Board that it was used in a few of their advertisements against the tax, was "blank check," which he sometimes expanded to "quickie blank check." That, he said, was what the Board of Education was asking for.

Out over the air on the last night of the campaign went Frank Wells's nasal voice to say things that supporters of the tax levy had no time to answer, for tomorrow the people would be going to the polls. He reviewed the history of the fight and said that when he and his friends first looked into the matter in April "we quickly found there was no budget available"—a statement that did not mislead anyone who had taken the trouble to investigate the facts. He implied that there was to be a raise of assessment of all property in the State—another reason, if it had been true, for voting against a tax-levy increase. When he got around to what an increase would cost the people of Pasadena, he talked only in total figures, and never mentioned the fact that even if the entire $0.45 additional were levied the first years—which no one had planned to do—the owner of a $10,000 house would pay only about $11.25 more a year in taxes. But Mr. Wells was speaking in larger terms. "Those camps and the revolutionary teaching," he cried, "would add hundreds of thousands to your tax bill." The fact that the summer camps for Pasadena children that he was talking about had never even been proposed to the Board—a joint lay-teachers' committee had simply looked into the idea—did not, apparently, disturb Mr. Wells.

"The city has long ago lost faith in the Board of Education," Mr. Wells at last said. "We have reached a low level in education. . . . We believe that the whole education system in Pasadena, its policies, its politics, what our children are taught and how they are taught, is at stake. We are asking that our children be taught well and wisely, with a maximum attention to the three R's, American history, geography and civil government; that they be schooled in their American heritage, taught real respect; and be thoroughly prepared to take their place in a competitive world. . . . Vote No tomorrow."

In the closing days of the campaign, other people and other forces had been just as busy, if not as well publicized or as verbose, as Mr. Wells. Louise Hawkes Padelford, suave and handsome, was usually on hand at important meetings to make a few remarks, many of them specifically directed against Federal Aid to Education. But her chief and most effective role was that of hostess at intimate lunches and gatherings at home where, with her customary graciousness and hospitality, she entertained those who, like her, were dissatisfied with Pasadena's school administration and wanted to discuss it in full. Cay Hallberg made some speeches against the tax election, even though she was still chiefly interested in getting rid of Willard Goslin. "But this is a democracy," she explained, "and when the School Development Council voted to fight the tax, I agreed to go along, although I thought at the time it was clouding the issue. . . ." The Property Owners Division of the Realty Board ran a series of outsize, outspoken ads: VOTE NO ON THE SCHOOL TAX INCREASE: WATCH YOUR POCKETBOOK.

The Administration itself was quietly disseminating some pamphlets and a mimeographed analysis of the budget, the tax, and what the increase would mean to the community. The analysis was forthright and contained all the facts. But the audience it reached was not large. The press paid no attention to it, nor did it make an attempt to dissect the budget and the tax for itself. Indeed, when asked why his paper had not supported the tax, or at least taken a stand on it, the managing editor of the *Star-News* said it had not been given enough information. This in itself was a surprising statement to many people who knew that the facts were readily available—if a newspaper would only go out and get them, as most newspapers always do.

June 2 dawned bright and clear and warm. Those who had had long experience with such elections soon saw that the citizens were marching to the polls in record numbers. In 1937, when the last tax election was held, some 5,500 persons got out and voted—slightly over 8 per cent of the registered voters. And now, thirteen years later, 32,242 residents of Pasadena and Altadena turned out—this time, 38 per cent of the electorate. It was more than twice as many people as had ever voted before in a school Board election.

That night, as the votes were counted under the careful, impartial supervision of Board Secretary Courtenay Monsen, something more than just a record vote was chalked up. For the first time in its existence, Pasadena had voted down an increase in school-system taxes, and by a resounding majority. Although 10,032 men and women had voted Yes—more people than had ever voted Yes in a school election before—22,210 had voted No.

12

Repercussions

The civic hangover which many Pasadenans got up with on the morning of June 3 was hardly relieved by the stark reality of problems confronting the schools. But first everyone who had been connected with the fight had something to say.

The Superintendent of Schools simply announced that "I'm disappointed in the outcome. . . . However, in the face of the vote of citizens of the community, there's no course ahead but to run the best schools we can on the 90 cent levy." President Wopschall promised that the Board "will do everything in our power to provide a good education for our children on a budget that will have to be cut some $385,000. Personally, I feel that it was a vote against the children of Pasadena." A spokesman for the Realty Board said, "We are immensely gratified with the support of the voters in this matter."

Frank Wells, speaking for himself and for his School Development Council, had the most to say, and what he said gave no indications that he and the SDC intended to take a back seat from now on. Mr. Wells knew he had won, and he made it clear that he was about to make the most of it.

"We are pleased and happy," he announced. ". . . We are also humble in the knowledge that while the Council did lead the campaign, success came because this was a movement of all the people against both the Administration and the curriculum. We fully realize our responsibility of leadership given us by the voters. . . . The Council and its thousands of backers are happiest because parents and taxpayers in the Pasadena School District have lost any former apathy. . . . We invite all parents to join us on the School Development Council—a group really representative of Pasadena's varying interests—as the election proved. . . . We will move at once to the voice of the people. . . ."

The most immediate result of the election was a city-wide movement to conduct a civilian survey into the school system. It had been engendered, apparently independently, on a number of fronts. The School Development Council, the Realty Board, and various organizations supporting the Goslin program at one time or another all suggested that such a survey would be useful. Five days after the election the Board of Education invited representatives of no less than seventy-five local organizations to meet with the Board to talk the thing over. Mr. Wopschall made it plain why he was asking so many. "The Board of Education and the Administration . . . [feel] that major problems facing the school system should receive the attention of as broad a base of public opinion as we are able to muster. . . . We feel that the school system is seriously jeopardized by existing community differences, and we need [your help] . . ." It was, Mr. Wopschall said, their purpose to "unite the community in support of its public school system, identify the purposes of education . . . [and] the strengths and weaknesses of the school program, the school organization, and its business practices; and to make recommendations for improvements."

On June 7 representatives of sixty organizations showed up, alphabetically composed of groups ranging from the Altadena Chamber of Commerce to Zonta International. Even this meeting, called in a peaceful moment after the dust of battle had settled, was not without its discord. A man named Edgar Thompson, now representing the Altadena Poppyfield Association but during the campaign the very effective press agent for the SDC, got up and objected to the way, in his opinion, the meeting was packed with groups which had duplicate memberships and had voted for the Goslin Administration, whereas "only four" of those invited to the meeting, including the School Development Council, had been against the tax and were really representative. It was, said Mr. Thompson, a case of "joiners against the people." When Frank Wells rose to speak, a heckler tried to halt him, but President Wopschall, maintaining democratic procedure, insisted he be allowed to read his statement. That statement contained a letter from an unidentified friend, and it urged the SDC to press for the removal of Willard Goslin and his immediate staff. And Mr. Wells himself, without identifying his source, told how he had heard rumors that both the Board and the superintendent were planning to resign if the election went against them, and darkly hinted that some people were even talking about a recall election to oust the Board.

The upshot of the meeting of the sixty was that each representative was asked to report to his organization and return in six weeks with a recommendation.

That same day—June 7—Willard Goslin submitted to the Board of Education a detailed letter outlining his proposals for cutting the elementary-school budget. He itemized a total deduction of $506,000. "We have deliberately developed a list that goes beyond the $398,000 figure," he said, so that the least harmful items could be selected. The Goslin list slashed all along the line. It placed kindergarten teachers back on two-a-day sessions, postponed the openings of several new buildings, cut out certain specialty teachers and some auxiliary services, reduced the undistributed reserve, and eliminated entirely the proposed recreational program.

This was tasty meat for Frank Wells, who at once came out with a statement charging the Goslin Administration with "vindictiveness" and with taking "revenge against the people." And, now that he had what he considered a mandate from the people, his School Development Council made its own proposals, embodying some of Kroeger's, some new ones of its own, and a few of the more obvious and irrefutable Goslin cuts. It upped the estimated amount to be received from assessments, slashed holes in Administrative costs and in the retirement fund for noncertified (nonteaching) employees, and with infinite shrewdness made its largest single cut simply by eliminating the general reserve, which, it said, was not needed. It was the kind of budget that might please everyone except those who were charged with implementing it, based as it was so largely on undocumented guesswork.

A week later the Board of Education and Mr. Goslin again came up with their own elementary-school budget. It followed the lines of Mr. Goslin's June 7 proposal, although it replaced part of the recreational fund, and a few other items down the list. As it finally emerged and was passed, slightly under $400,000 was excised from the preelection preliminary figure. And so at last, with little attention paid to the proposals of the

School Development Council, the budget controversy was laid to rest.

The proposed school survey had meanwhile become a focal point in the city. In all, thirty-five of the original sixty civic bodies came forth with recommendations of one kind or another. Some, like the one presented by PTA Council President Maren Fulton, who had labored so diligently for passage of the tax levy, were detailed and all-inclusive. Pointedly, Mrs. Fulton suggested, among other things, that "No one group or special interest should dominate the planning or selection of the staff" to be appointed. The Citizens' Council for Planning proposed that leading educators in the State name a committee to make the study. The Pasadena Council of Churches, a staunch supporter of the Goslin régime, admitted that the school system had been weak in its public relations—a statement with which no one could quarrel—but asked that "there be no basic changes in personnel or program . . . unless and until a clear need for such changes is indicated by an impartial and comprehensive survey."

The Board of Education dutifully waded through every proposal and finally decided that its best bet was for the Board itself to name an impartial committee composed of leading and irreproachable Pasadena citizens who would study the needs of the schools and come up with a report. The Board's announcement was followed by one dissenting vote, which was backed by the SDC. That vote was cast by the Chamber of Commerce, which asked that a nonprofit corporation be formed to contract with the Board to study the system, and then remain as a permanent watchdog over the operation of the schools. This the Board would not do, and when its own Survey Committee was formed and began operating, the Chamber went along with it.

Of the thirteen men and women originally asked to serve, only two refused, both of them because of press of private affairs. As finally constituted, the Survey Committee was indeed representative of the community. Named as chairman was a personable, capable lawyer named James Boyle, and among its leading members were the able president of the California Institute of Technology, Lee DuBridge; President John S. Moore of the Pasadena Realty Board, which had so forcefully opposed the tax rise; an enterprising contractor named Edward A. Lockett; and that staunch protagonist of Pro America and the School Development Council, Louise Hawkes Padelford. These members first met with the Board of Education at a luncheon in the Huntington Hotel, at which Mr. Wopschall, speaking for the Board, promised them a free hand. Although he did not try to limit the survey with a time schedule, he told them the Board would like to have the survey completed early the following spring—the spring of 1951—so that it could be studied and publicized and activated before the time for another tax election rolled around in June. However, many things happened between that August day and the next June to slow up the committee's work, and to bring in a fresh set of circumstances for the committee to examine.

13

"An Ideological Investigation"

Having got in its postelection licks on the proposed budget cutting, the School Development Council next turned its attention to more esoteric matters. On July 11 it addressed a five-page "open letter" (copies to Pasadena and Los Angeles newspapers) to the Board of Education. It was signed by the Executive Committee of the SDC, and it presented two main requests: (1) "an ideological investigation of curriculum, methods and personnel within the Pasadena School District . . ." and (2) loyalty oaths "by administrators and teachers within the . . . District, stipulating dismissal for those who refused to sign." And for good measure it also suggested that oaths be signed "by all citizens engaged in active or advisory work for the System."

The Executive Committee's letter had a great deal to say about some familiar subjects—William Heard Kilpatrick, "the Columbia Cult" of progressive educators, and the evils of Progressive Education itself. It also had some suggestions to make and some provocative questions to ask, and it wanted urgent action and answers on all of them.

One of the letter's most startling suggestions was that "Over and above the present planned survey [then already under discussion, and soon formed] we . . . ask the Board to determine immediately the politico-social aims of the present school administration—in curriculum, methods, and personnel, both of District, staff and guest lecturers. . . . We suggest that such patriotic organizations as the American Legion and Sons and Daughters of the American Revolution be called upon to direct [*sic*] or actively assist the Board in the study."

The committee's ideological questions were no less arresting. Quoting from a school-system handbook on "Audio-Visual Education," the letter asked "the ideological investigators to determine what kind of thinking is meant when the book states that one 'objective of the course . . . is understanding why democracy has often failed in the past (in this case, Rome).' Has the Board or the general public EVER thought of Rome as a democracy? A primitive, limited Republic—perhaps. A representative democracy like the United States of America? Never! Then why the insinuation that 'democracy has often failed in the past'? with Rome as an example? Is this part of a campaign to 'sell' our children on the collapse of our way of life and substitution of collectivism?"

From the same book the letter quoted out of context a reference to "The Star-Spangled Banner" to try to prove that the book's authors considered it a warmongering song. The letter gave a totally inaccurate and misleading account of a school meeting where a speaker, they claimed, had "repudiated" both the Constitution and the Bill of Rights. Finally, it made the flat statement that the above "and many other instances, too numerous to mention," were gravely alarming to "parents and taxpayers of the School Development Council."

To the relief of the school Board and Mr. Goslin, the matter of the loyalty oath, which might have developed into a red-hot issue had it been permitted to burn long, was got rid of at once. For a change, the habit the local press had of printing in full all the SDC statements and communications paid off to the Administration's advantage. The day after the SDC letter was read in meeting and published in the *Star-News* and *Independent*, the Pasadena Education Association, representing most of the system's teachers, called its members into a hasty session and there reaffirmed, in public and for the benefit of the now-noxious SDC, their own loyalty oath, and called on all other teachers to do so at once.

The rest of the letter was not so easily disposed of. On July 20 a first draft of a reply was prepared for the approval of Mr. Goslin and the Board. It pulled no punches. It stated that there was no reason why "the general survey which will soon be inaugurated" could not do the job the SDC would like to turn over to the American Legion and other patriotic societies. It asked the SDC please to specify where Pasadena's school system was "incompatible" with the goals the SDC had listed. It demanded that the SDC redefine its vague references to "Experience Curriculum," "Common Learning," and "Core." It asked for some indication of real dissatisfaction "at the classroom level." As for Kilpatrick, it said: "The fact that Mr. Kilpatrick has been influential in education in no way means that Mr. Goslin, members of the Board of Education, or anyone else, wholeheartedly subscribe to what Mr. Kilpatrick, or anyone else, believes. Again, please spell out what you consider to be unwholesome influences. . . ."

Finally, in reply to the SDC's blunt question asking whether the system's program was "part of a campaign to 'sell' our children on the collapse of our way of life and substitution of collectivism," it said: "We believe you are out of order even to ask such a question. . . . However, for your information, the members of the Board, the Administration, and our schoolteachers are just as enthusiastic about the American way of life as you are. . . ."

But this draft was never sent. Mr. Goslin and others decided it would have little effect, and, also, they questioned whether a letter such as the SDC's should be dignified with a reply. However, and perhaps ill advisedly, a watered-down version was finally written and dispatched on August 15. This version was more general, and aside from a few ironies which might have passed over the heads of the more literal-minded members of the Executive Committee, it said little. And it was by no means satisfactory to the committee. On September 5 they again sent a have-you-stopped-beating-your-wife-answer-yes-or-no communication, sharply taking the Board to task for failing to answer the questions previously asked. The questions were asked again, along with some brand-new ones. And this letter contained something else that was new, for it was signed not by Frank Wells, but by W. Ernest Brower.

In August of 1950 Dr. Ernest Brower was just about as little known to the members of the school Board as his predecessor Frank Wells had been six months before. Who Dr. Brower was, what caused him to join the SDC, and why he was now its chairman, was a story of some significance.

Dr. Brower is an osteopath. He was born and raised in Pasadena, attended its public schools, and graduated from the College of Osteopathic Physicians and Surgeons in Los Angeles—

an institution with an excellent reputation. Now forty-seven and with lucrative practice, Ernest Brower lives in a comfortable pastel pink house in a well-to-do section of Altadena. He is on the short side, his gray hair tends to be bushy, and his mouth is small and firm. When he laughs, he does so briefly and almost soundlessly.

Aside from his practice, Dr. Brower's main activity is fighting what he conceives to be an ever widening and baleful Communist influence in practically all public schools in the United States—all schools, that is, which could in any way be described as tainted with Progressive leanings. His daughter Gwendolyn, now sixteen, had gone to a Pasadena elementary school, and, by her father's own account, learned so little and that little so badly that she was sent to a local private school. But she yearned for the companionship of her old friends and, in 1948—"the same time Goslin came to town"—she returned to the public schools. Her father soon regretted the step. She came home, he said, interested in nothing but happiness and security. She wanted to go with "the herd." She even called policemen "cops," and it was that sort of disrespect for public institutions he didn't like. All of this so disturbed Dr. Brower that he felt impelled to join the ranks of the School Development Council. He became convinced, before long, that teaching in Pasadena was "leading to Socialism, and there isn't much difference between Socialism and Communism." Dr. Brower voices his convictions with undiluted force. He disapproves of teaching sex in the schools to teen-age mixed classes because, he feels, that leads to free love and free love leads to Communism. He has recently expressed himself as seeing evidences, in the United States, of the same trend toward Socialism and Communism that some of his friends saw at firsthand in Yugoslavia and China. When reminded that the United States still has representative government elected by the people, Dr. Brower once replied that he was most fearful that the education children were receiving would eventually lead them to elect the wrong kind of congressmen.

During the spring and summer of 1950, after Dr. Brower had been vice chairman of the SDC for some months, the organization found itself in the middle of an internecine war behind the façade of unity it exposed to public view. Like many such organizations, the aims of its members were beginning to differ in degree and in kind. Mrs. Cay Hallberg, for example, had never made any bones about what she wanted. Glenn Ebersole, its first president, who had almost been forgotten in the subsequent shuffle, went along pretty much with Mrs. Hallberg's desire to get Mr. Goslin out, and he also felt that teaching in Pasadena simply was not very good. John Petterson, who had been so active in the tax campaign and had no children, apparently was more interested in Americanism. Everyone knew where Dr. Brower stood. But Frank Wells, according to some of his former associates, seemed to think that he, having contributed so much to winning the tax fight, should continue to represent the Council and, as its head, he demanded that he be given blanket authority to ask for the resignation both of Mr. Goslin and of the school Board.

The first person of consequence in the organization to take issue with him was Mrs. Hallberg. It was her honest opinion, which she has reiterated with perfect frankness many times since, that more could be got by working *with* the school Board than against it. When an abortive attempt was made to collect recall-petition signatures, soon after the June election, Mrs. Hallberg objected and resigned from the School Development Council. This she did without any public fuss, and her name disappeared from the local newspapers where it had of late been printed so frequently. However, she continued to go about the chief job she had assigned herself. One of her main activities, the precise effectiveness of which can never be measured, was conducting several group meetings with some of her non-SDC friends and at least two Board members, Lawrence Lamb and Milton Wopschall, where she drove home her opposition to "modern pragmatic education."

The School Development Council's private little war went on for about two months after the tax election, and its details are now sunk in a morass of charges and countercharges. Two of Mrs. Wells's colleagues have since told the story that after he asked blanket authority to demand the resignation of Willard Goslin and the Board, his Executive Committee first voted him such authority, and then, at a later meeting, flatly rescinded it and ousted him. When confronted with this story, Mr. Wells was somewhat evasive. He admitted, smiling his amiable smile, that some of the details were true but that others were not. Be that as it may, on August 3 the School Development Council, in a shower of pleasantries, announced that it had accepted Frank Wells's resignation so that he could devote more time to his business. "We fear we shall have to search long," the statement said, "to find a president who can match the personal sacrifice of time and money and the untiring, devoted and able leadership Frank Wells gave the Council." At the same time, it announced that Dr. Brower, who had been first vice president, would now become acting chairman.

It was only two days after he took office that Dr. Brower sent his own probing letter to the Pasadena Board of Education. And once more the Board took its time replying, probably because Mr. Goslin took *his* time preparing the facts for the letter. But when the Board did reply, over the signature of President Wopschall, it came out and said what many people wanted to say. It gave a long and detailed answer to the Rome versus Democracy query, explaining: "It seems wise to have children know why democracies have failed in the past so that this country will not make the mistakes which have sometimes destroyed or warped democracy." It proved to the satisfaction of anyone who could read plain English that "The Star-Spangled Banner" tale was a flagrant distortion of the facts; the book had simply suggested that, during the showing of an educational film, the teacher play "The Star-Spangled Banner" or "any popular war song" as a means of entertaining the students while changing reels.

The letter then responded to a number of questions concerning Kilpatrick as an educator, declaring that the schools' teachers would continue to use his recorded lectures and published texts. In answer to Dr. Brower's question, "Does the Administration agree with the socialistic philosophy of Professor William Heard Kilpatrick?" the letter said succinctly, "The Board of Education and the Administration do not agree with any socialistic philosophy." Dr. Brower's letter also made an issue of Mary Beauchamp, who had already resigned and left Pasadena. Dr. Brower claimed she had "resigned under fire" and wanted to know if "her influence on our schools" had been ended, "or has she left behind an organization designed to perpetuate and accelerate the Kilpatrick philosophy in our schools?" "Miss Beauchamp," the Board replied, "did not resign under fire, nor has she left any 'organization' behind her."

By the time the school Board's answer was in the mail, the patience of many people on all sides was wearing out, and, although the community still seemed peaceful, anti-Administration forces were at work up and down the line.

14

The Situation Deteriorates

By the fall of 1950, despite the election setback, Willard Goslin had made much satisfactory progress with his educational program. Over a hundred men and women—teachers, would-be teachers, administrators, and parents—had attended the five-week session of the second summer workshop, spending their time in study groups, going to lectures, listening to advice on individual projects, doing research in the library, and so on, through the intricacies of teacher training. Although for better or for worse Mary Beauchamp had resigned and gone East, Mr. Goslin had the kind of staff he wanted. In addition to Dr. Gilchrist, Stuart Marsee, and Blair Nixon, he had a few others, such as young Franklin Patterson, who by now was a full-time curriculum coordinator, and a smart, knowing educator named Jane Hood, whom the superintendent had borrowed from the University of Southern California, where she had run the Human Relations Workshop. She also was to be a curriculum coordinator. That summer too, in conjunction with San Diego County and Long Beach, the system had instituted a child-study project at a place called Camp Hi-Hill under the direction of a famous child psychologist named Prescott. And, just before the fall term opened, the Central Office staff, along with a few representatives from the teaching staff who went along as their guests, had its second annual three-day conference—this time at Arrowhead Springs. Like its predecessor, it was agreed to have been very successful.

But beneath the surface of this seemingly smooth-flowing stream of scholastic activity there were, by now, strong and swift undercurrents of dissatisfaction. Naturally enough, the Administration's defeat in the tax election had been a bitter blow, and after it the Board of Education seemed to feel it had suffered a loss of prestige. Just as naturally, no one was particularly pleased with the persistent outcries of the School Development Council, by now so vociferous that, as Mr. Goslin said at a Board meeting, more and more of the town's citizens were beginning to think there really was something suspect about the public schools.

Then, too, Mr. Goslin was running into trouble with the Board itself. At the time he hired Jane Hood as curriculum coordinator, he had been privately warned that some people in Pasadena might object to her because she had run a Human Relations Workshop at USC, and that meant mixing the races, which was an abomination to so many of the old guard. The fact that some of these people had gone so far as to telephone several Board members, warning them against hiring her, hadn't made selling the Board on her appointment any easier.

Although the disagreements that followed were hardly earth-shaking in themselves, several made local news, and all were symptomatic of the temper of the times in Pasadena and indicative of the Board's increasing uneasiness.

The first full-dress disagreement between Mr. Goslin and the Board came about when the Administration presented the

Board with a bill for $600 for the system's share of the costs of the Prescott Child Study Conference held the previous August. Although some of Mr. Goslin's administrators maintained that the Board had, at a summer conference meeting, been told briefly about the plan for this two-week study, the Board's members acted very surprised and displeased when they were confronted with the bill. They claimed they had never been consulted and felt their prerogatives had been badly bruised. Mr. Goslin's assistants took the blame for not having put the thing more formally before the Board; Mr. Goslin himself felt that, in any event, he was in line with the stipulations set forth in his original letter to the Board before he took the job—that this was the sort of expense not needing Board approval. Two County Council rulings were obtained, one stating that the expense was justified without consulting the Board, and the other saying just the reverse. In the end, the Board, after acrimonious debate, voted unanimously to approve payment. Miss Sterling, however, said she did so against her better judgment, and severely criticized both the superintendent and the Prescott study. "I am voting for this report now," she said, "because I do not want to embarrass the Long Beach and San Diego school districts. . . ."

A few days later Lawrence Lamb let his long-smouldering resentment of what *he* considered usurpation of Board authority burst into flame. His somewhat vague complaint had to do with the field of public relations. "It'll be like making them 'eat crow,' " he said, "but the city school administrators have got to concentrate on the teaching and leave public relations to the Board of Education. . . . We must again resume our leadership. . . . We must never again delegate it to others and relegate ourselves to the 'amen corner.' " Mr. Lamb was especially incensed, he let it be known, at the "outside crew" Mr. Goslin had brought in and seemed to think they had a "free hand." It was obvious that Mr. Lamb did not intend to concern himself with that conditonal letter of acceptance written before he had become a member of the Board, wherein Mr. Goslin outlined what he insisted would be the superintendent's privileges in matters precisely like this one.

Another dispute arose over the appointment of a Hungarian-born young man named George Gerbner, whom the superintendent had brought from one of the schools, where he was a teacher, to be part-time curriculum assistant and to continue part-time as an instructor in journalism. He had once been a reporter on the San Francisco *Chronicle,* and during the war he had edited an Army paper before he became an Office of Strategic Services paratrooper and underground agent. So he was also asked to edit an intraoffice public-relations pamphlet called the *Clearing House,* an outgrowth of the Arrowhead Springs Conference. It was to be a two-way transmission belt of information, suggestions, and criticisms to and from teachers. When George Gerbner's name was presented for Board approval, Mr. Lamb, again with public relations in mind, strenuously objected—first because he said that Gerbner was only to be an "errand boy" for the Administration, and second because he thought it was "dishonest" for the Administration to name him curriculum assistant when it planned to use him for public relations. Harriet Sterling concurred, and the result was a 3-2 vote for Gerbner's approval. It was the first open split on a Goslin appointment.

Some of this antagonism of the Board might have been caused by something that Willard Goslin had said at the Arrowhead Conference and that at once found its way back to the members. At Arrowhead, during a long speech covering the gamut of education problems in Pasadena, Mr. Goslin was discussing at one point the Survey Committee and the Board's relation to it. "The Board of Education," he said "(and I would prefer that they were here this morning), from the viewpoint of the community has been over the past year or two or three a relatively weak board. . . . They say so themselves." What Mr. Goslin said later on in his speech, but what did *not* get back to the Board, was that he meant the Board was weak in the eyes of the community in the same way that he felt his own Administration was weak—that a combination of circumstances such as the shortcomings of the system in the last days of the Sexson régime, the heated outbursts of the School Development Council, the defeat over the tax election, and kindred matters made an independent survey a welcome and necessary thing. And he had gone on to say: "Out of that background I think this Board has done a magnificent job; under pressure and fire they have matured as a Board as rapidly as I have seen any group mature, and I have dealt with several under some rather trying circumstances." That did not get back to the Board either; all they heard, in effect, was that they were "weak."

When he returned from Arrowhead and got wind that the Board was upset—Miss Sterling and Lawrence Lamb were reported to be "hopping mad"—he at once sat down with them and ran off a tape recording of the entire speech. It did little good; the damage had been done.

While relations worsened between Mr. Goslin and his Board, other matters began to assume serious proportions on another front. Mr. Goslin had long known that a tight little corps of administrators in the system was unhappy with its lot, each man for one or another personal reason. Some were jealous because they had been passed over for jobs in favor of other men, some were nettled because they felt they should have been given better jobs when the new Administration took over, and some never made it clear why they were discontented. In any case, by the time the 1950 fall term was under way, word had filtered through the system that these dissidents were plotting to get rid of the superintendent. Even when, months later, their names were known to everyone connected with Pasadena schools, the entire active group never numbered more than six or eight men. Although they undoubtedly had a few other sympathizers in the heat of Goslin's last days, it was always these few who were named over and over again as the spear-head of the inside-the-system attack on Willard Goslin. No publicity ever got out about what they were doing or saying, but it appeared evident, by October, that their objections to the superintendent—objections mainly based, it seemed, on what they termed his high-handed ways and his uncooperative manner—had reached the now receptive ears of some Board members. But Mr. Goslin was still busy running the school system, and either did not or would not recognize the under-current of dissention stemming from a small group.

To comprehend the course of events that followed next, it is necessary to understand that Pasadena, with its traditionally conservative background, was (and still is) dominated, in the main, by a group of influential downtowners, most of them with big real-estate interests, whose social center was a place called the Overland Club and who pulled a great many strings in the operation of the city. It is quite true that many important Pasadenans have never been considered a part of this group—many industrialists and scientists, lawyers, bankers, and, in fact, most of the new Survey Committee investigating the schools—people who had a broad-based and deep interest in the welfare of the city. But the so-called "downtowners" had made it their business to control, collectively, as much of the city's activities as they could. These people, for obvious reasons, abhorred any rise in taxes, especially real-estate taxes. And, much as they welcomed new industry as a means of bringing in new revenue, they abhorred the social changes new industries create—particularly the influx of nonwhites who must be housed, fed, their children educated, and absorbed into the community. In times of stress, the more conservative of these landed gentry found their fears aggravated and their conservatism exaggerated to an abnormal degree.

The two newspapers in Pasadena, each in its own way, gave vast support to Downtown Pasadena, and by so doing gave vast support to opponents of the school system. The extreme antagonism which the *Independent* displayed in its fight against Willard Goslin and Progressive Education was obviously a boon to these conservative elements, who could sit quietly back and watch their battle being fought for them. Another boon was the play the *Star-News* and the *Independent* both gave to Frank Wells and Ernest Brower and the School Development Council, without ever telling anything about either man or attempting to define the motivation behind the Council. (With William Blair still keeping to his old policy of not discussing Board or other local affairs in his column, the only man on the *Star-News* who fought the battle on Willard Goslin's side was Chuck Perlee, an able and intelligent columnist and critic.) The public had suddenly found itself confronted with these forces against the schools, and was never given any background on which to judge those forces and decide whether what they were doing and saying was right.

As the fall term wore on, rumors spread like brush fire through the school system. The most persistent was that some members of the Overland group had baldly told several members of the Board they would give the next tax election, once more up for a vote the following June, no support whatsoever if Willard Goslin was still superintendent. This rumor gave rise to another: that some Board members were already having private talks among themselves to evolve ways and means to get Mr. Goslin out.

Although no public mention was made of it, the Board's first concerted break with Mr. Goslin came about the middle of October, when President Wopschall invited his fellow members to a luncheon at his house. The only person absent who would have been there had it been an ordinary gathering was Secretary Monsen. That noontime, over salad, it was suggested that the superintendent was getting out of hand and that perhaps they had better do something about it. This news came as a complete surprise to Mrs. Rinehart, who had stood firmly behind Willard Goslin and his Administration from the beginning. But others seemed to be in no such need of enlightenment, and that was the last Mrs. Rinehart was to hear about plans to ask for Mr. Goslin's resignation until the afternoon of November 8.

In the meantime, however, there emerged from the welter of rumors one incident indicating that some people were well aware of what was going on. About November 1, Mrs. Padelford was getting ready to go East to visit her father in New Jersey. A few days before, at a meeting of the Survey Committee, Mrs. Padelford was bidding her fellow members goodbye. "Well," she said gayly, "if the Board asks the superintendent to resign, I guess we can all relax, because then we won't need a survey after all." The other committee members were completely taken aback. Not only did they know nothing about anyone's plan to ask Mr. Goslin to resign; they disagreed with Louise Padelford most vehemently. Any change in the Administration would only make the need for a survey that much more imperative. As one of them afterward wryly observed, the survey was not planned as a means of getting Willard Goslin out of Pasadena.

On November 4 Willard Goslin flew East to attend a meeting of one of the commissions of the American Council on Education in Washington—a commission headed by Harvard's James B. Conant; and then he was going on to New York to attend a session of the National Citizens Commission for the Public Schools. Meanwhile, back in Pasadena, the clouds which not long ago had seemed no bigger than a man's hand had now gathered into a giant thunderhead which was soon to explode over the city.

At four-thirty on the afternoon of Tuesday, November 7, the Board of Education held its regular meeting in the conference room. The meeting was without incident until it neared its close. Then representatives of eight of Pasadena's schools stepped forward and handed Secretary Monsen a series of letters signed by 194 teachers and principals of their schools. All the letters had the same theme: they wished to endorse the Goslin Administration; they objected to the "attacks" being made on Mr. Goslin and his Administration; and they wished to express their faith and confidence in the Board of Education. The letters obviously represented a group effort to stem the tide against Mr. Goslin. But Milton Wopschall would permit none of the letters to be read aloud. They were, as usual, filed for consideration by the Board.

At the same meeting the Board also received an "unofficial" letter from a Central Office administrator charging that the pro-Goslin letters had been signed under pressure. Although this communication was not made public that day at all, its contents had leaked to the press by nightfall.

At last the controversy over Willard Goslin was out in the open—and Willard Goslin was in New York.

15

Mr. Goslin Gets a Telegram

Early on the morning of Thursday, November 9, the telephone rang in Willard Goslin's room at the Barbizon-Plaza. It was the desk calling. They had a telegram for Mr. Goslin; could they send it up? Mr. Goslin said they could. When the boy knocked, Mr. Goslin opened the door, took the telegram, and tipped the boy a quarter. Then, still in his pajamas, he sat down on the edge of the bed and read the wire. It was very long. This is what it said:

At Tuesday's Board meeting various teachers' groups presented signed testimonials approving the curriculum policies and school program of the Administration. These testimonials are admittedly a direct outgrowth of the activities of the Public Relations Committee of the Pasadena Education Association. The soliciting of signatures for these petitions has in reality caused a deep rift within the teaching and administrative ranks. Many teachers and administrators are signing because they feel it is necessary to protect their position with the Administration. Others are refusing on principle to sign and this group feels sure that they have irretrievably lost face with the Administration. There is, therefore, added to the deep division in the community this real division among employees.

We have been contacted by many employees whom we consider

are among the most professional and substantial in the system. They feel that we are now in a position from which we cannot recover. Many of the school employees will from this point on consider themselves as part of the opposition and will be co-operating with the opposition in such a way as to make any recovery or harmony impossible.

We are interested mainly, as you know, in promoting and continuing a fine educational system in Pasadena. We are of the opinion that the school system is suffering and will continue to suffer because of the lack of harmony within the system itself, as well as in the community as a whole. We feel that the possibilities of winning a tax election are becoming remote and that the school system will suffer real hardships in all phases of its program if we cannot supply it with adequate financing.

In our opinion the main controversy in Pasadena settles itself around you as an individual and therefore it becomes our very sad duty to suggest to you, in accordance with your own statement to the Board that if the situation became untenable you would volunteer to step out, that you resign because we no longer feel that the situation can be resolved.

We regret that the urgency of the situation has caused us to take this means of informing you of our conclusion. We would have preferred an across the table conference but we know that the opposition will not wait for us as they have plans to meet your plane with a demand for your resignation. Such a demand would continue to deepen the rift both in the system and in the community until election day with the end result that the schools would continue to suffer. We also feel that you might be in a better position professionally if you would tender your resignation before demands can be made upon you in force.

If you feel that you would like to have additional time in the East, we on the Board will be glad to authorize an extension of your trip.

The telegram was signed:

"Milton Wopschall, Lawrence Lamb, Harriet Sterling, Vernon Brydolf, Mrs. Rinehart present but not concurring."

Should they care to take the time to examine it closely, students of good literature, students of good manners, and students of democratic procedure will, without question, find the Board's telegram a source of much interesting material. It was, like a brand of watered-down cheap whisky, a curious blend. It was contradictory and paradoxical; it contained some elements of *Alice in Wonderland,* some elements of the dime novel, and some elements of the embarrassed schoolboy who has been caught writing on the back fence.

The fact that the telegram was sent at all has mystified a great many Pasedenans from the day it was first made public. The Board knew very well that Mr. Goslin was not in permanent residence in New York, as the closing gratuitous offer to "authorize an extension" of his trip testified so clearly. Even more mysterious was the ludicrous reason expressed in the wire itself: the "opposition" was threatening to meet Mr. Goslin's plane and demand his resignation. To this day no one has ever been able to identify the "opposition," or to give the name of anyone planning to be at the airport. Some people hinted that it was to be members of the School Development Council, but the School Development Council categorically denies this charge. It says, in turn, that the delegation was to consist of a handful of disgruntled schoolteachers, but this has also been denied on all sides.

Whoever it might have been, if anyone, the Board subsequently was never able to explain satisfactorily why *any* opposition group should so intimidate a duly elected body which was responsible to all the citizens of Pasadena. For such a body of grownups to explain its action on the grounds that the delegation at the plane "would continue to deepen the rift" seemed to many people flimsy and ill founded. As someone later wrote in to inquire, with neat logic, "if the Board was afraid of having anyone meet Mr. Goslin's plane, why didn't they tell him to take a different one?"

The Board's seemingly inconsistent approach to the pro-Goslin teachers versus the anti-Goslin teachers, as mentioned in the wire, was equally baffling to many. No one denies that, after Mr. Goslin went off to New York early in November, a group of admirers in the Pasadena Education Association, disturbed by the flow of rumors running throughout the system, took it into their own hands—without Mr. Goslin's knowledge—to circulate petitions which affirmed their confidence in their boss and what he was doing. Their right to do so, despite Mr. Wopschall's strong objection to it, seemed plain. What was hard to understand was the Board's objecting, in its wire, to this "soliciting of signatures" in favor of Mr. Goslin while at the same time it condoned, in effect, the action of those who were against such soliciting.

Overshadowing all these questions was, of course, the demand for Mr. Goslin's resignation itself. And that too was explained on what turned out to be just as mysterious and vague grounds. His contract had a year and a half to run. The school Board had never sat down with him to discuss, in detail or even with generalities, the "rift" in the system and in the community. It had never told him that it felt that any future tax increase could not be passed so long as he was superintendent. Soon after the joint Administration-school-Board defeat of the tax election, Willard Goslin had met in his office for a long heart-to-heart talk with all Board members, and had explored the whole field of problems now ahead of them. He warned that it would be rough sledding at times, and he knew that it would be the Administration that would have to do the dirty work, and that any step the Board wanted him to take he would take. He had not mentioned resigning; certainly he would have offered to get out had they talked their problems over with him and found that the Administration and the Board could never come to a mutually satisfactory agreement for their settlement. But this the Board had never done in all the months that followed, and for its members to believe that he had volunteered "to step out" without any such cards-on-table talks, without any attempt at first arriving at some solutions, indicated in what low regard the Board held ordinary business practices and procedures. Furthermore, at the end of that meeting in the superintendent's office, they had expressed complete confidence in what he had done and was doing. They had then still been in the fight together.

Questioned individually, various members of the Board have since given varying explanations as to why they no longer wanted Willard Goslin in Pasadena. Lawrence Lamb was most explicit. The whole reason they asked Mr. Goslin to resign, he explains sweepingly, was that they thought his Administration was a failure. "He didn't evaluate the community," says Mr. Lamb. "He didn't *take* time—put that down: he didn't *take* time. He *had* the time. And people couldn't understand what he was talking about. He didn't have the right rapproach—that's the word, *rapproach,* to the grass-roots problem."

Milton Wopschall walked around the subject and arrived at

a conclusion from several different points of view. He says he thinks "something happened" to Mr. Goslin during two years in Pasadena. "He was," says Mr. Wopschall, "like an evangelist"—a statement with which no one could quarrel: in a manner of speaking, he had always been one. Mr. Wopschall also objected to the fact that the superintendent never put members of the school Board on lay-teacher committees—a procedure that Mr. Goslin had always been against because he thought that the Board should represent all the community and not segments of it. Mr. Wopschall, too, made quite a point of the "summer camps," thereby unwittingly keeping company with extreme right wingers of the School Development Council. (This was a matter to which many Goslin opponents seemed to have attached undue importance in view of the nebulous state of the summer-camp idea at the time of the flare-up, and in view of the harmlessness of the idea itself.) And Mr. Wopschall has complained: "Willard thinks nationally, and not locally. What we need solved here are the Pasadena school-system's problems. We aren't interested in what is going on in other places."

Harriet Sterling's main reason seemed to center around the familiar theme of Mr. Goslin's "failure" to take the Board into his confidence—a theme expressed by others also, although the record seems to indicate that he did so on all matters where the Board's confidence was needed; and again on that subject he had made himself unequivocally clear when he first and conditionally accepted the job. Miss Sterling also seemed to feel that he was too much of a zealot; and, too, that he was "bored" with social affairs. Following up objections she voiced in Board meetings, she has since complained bitterly about the Prescott

Conference affair and the appointment of George Gerbner. They seemed to rankle deep within her.

Although Vernon Brydolf, the oldest member of the Board in point of time served, has privately expressed himself around town, he has refused to grant interviews on the subject, and does not wish to be quoted. His feeling in the matter was best indicated by his stated desire that the whole thing should be dropped and forgotten, and that the schools should now get on with the business at hand. As a solid member of the community, and for a long while a staunch supporter of Willard Goslin, Mr. Brydolf surprised many a fellow citizen when he not only failed to support the man he had championed less than three years ago, but actually joined in requesting his resignation.

The member of the Board who remained steadfastly loyal to Willard Goslin and to all his policies was, as the wire itself proved, Mrs. Gladys Rinehart. Having very much of a mind of her own, she has always stuck by her guns when she believed she was right, even when, as the wife of a conservative and substantial citizen, she was leaving herself open to accusations of playing ball with what some extremists called "subversive" and "Communistic" elements. And her attitude certainly did not make life on the Board much easier during those last hectic days. Because she had to play her part alone, she was seldom consulted in advance on Board matters, as the others were. And, as has been observed, after the lunch at Milton Wopschall's she heard nothing more about the plan to ask for Mr. Goslin's resignation until she walked into the special Board meeting and found the first draft of the wire prepared and ready for discussion. Everything she said that day was to no avail—even her strong and pointed reference to the Survey Committee which the Board itself had appointed to study the entire school system so thoroughly. Why not wait, Mrs. Rinehart wanted to know, until this body had finished its work? But Mrs. Rinehart's voice was unheeded and, for all practical purposes, unheard.

Willard Goslin sat on the edge of the bed in the Barbizon-Plaza and read the telegram several times. His first feeling was one of shock. That was followed by one of depression. Mr. Goslin is an honest man, and a trusting one. That this sort of thing should happen—not necessarily to him, but to any self-respecting person—was bewildering and rather frightening.

It was still early in the morning; it was three hours earlier in California. Mr. Goslin shaved and bathed and dressed, and went downstairs for breakfast; then he called his wife in Pasadena, and told her the news. Her reaction was calm and cheering. Then he telephoned his assistant superintendent, Dr. Gilchrist, asked him to put Mrs. Greeson on another extension, and read the wire to them. Next, he asked Dr. Gilchrist and Dr. Marsee to go to Milton Wopschall and Vernon Brydolf and tell them that, unless the Board released the wire at once to the teachers and the press, he would release it himself. He felt that the teachers in particular had a right to know what was going on. That done, Mr. Goslin sent a telegram to Mr. Wopschall, acknowledging the Board's wire, saying that he would "discuss the matter with you when I return to Pasadena on Monday," and advising the Board president that in the meantime the Messrs. Gilchrist and Marsee would represent him.

That day Willard Goslin wound up his affairs in New York

by attending sessions of the National Citizens Commission for the Public Schools. He said nothing about the wire. That night he flew to St. Louis to keep a long-standing date he had with his brother to shoot quail. Next day he got his limit—ten birds.

That night he flew back to Pasadena.

16

Turmoil in Pasadena

The editor and the managing editor of the *Independent* and a reporter from the *Star-News* had sat in on the private Board of Education meeting the day it was decided to ask Willard Goslin for his resignation. These gentlemen had agreed to keep the story under their hats in the hope that the superintendent would be willing to bow out quietly, which is what the Board was most anxious for him to do. And so, when Mr. Goslin had so uncooperatively asked that the telegram be made public, the press was ready to print the news. This it did on Friday, November 10.

It hit a great many people in town with all the stunning impact of a hurricane. Despite the weeks of rumors inside the school system, despite the persistent backstairs talk among a privileged few who had an "in" with those who knew what was going on, not many townsfolk were aware that anything like this was brewing. But now that the word was out, support for Willard Goslin, however belated, came from some most unexpected quarters.

In his living room before dinner that Friday night, an industrialist named Philip Fogg got to thinking about what he had just read in the *Star-News.* Philip Fogg can accurately be described as a leading, and a most conservative, citizen of Pasadena. He is president of the Consolidated Engineering Corporation, a well established concern manufacturing electronic instruments. He was once president of the Pasadena Chamber of Commerce, and is now president of the local Rotary. He had been invited to serve on the Survey Committee studying the school system (an invitation he had been forced to decline because of his war-contract work), and he himself had two sons in an Altadena elementary school. He had come to know and admire Willard Goslin through their mutual interest in Rotary. And now, like many other thinking citizens, what had happened to Pasadena's superintendent startled and angered him.

That same day the same feeling stirred to activity a number of other conservative members of the community. One of them was Mrs. William E. Hansen, a blond and bright mother of two daughters in the schools, an energetic woman who has long been active in such projects as the City Planning Commission, the Council of Social Agencies, and the Women's Civic League, the last two of which she had in the past served as president. Another was J. Lowell McAdam, the head of a construction company who had been the 1949 chairman of the local Community Chest. Still another was a young radiologist named Robert Freeman, whose late father had been one of Pasadena's best-known and best-loved ministers.

Before long these people, together with a number of others, had decided to do something about the Goslin matter. Dr. Freeman began rounding up his friends—he called Betty Hansen and Lowell McAdam and Philip Fogg. Other people with the same idea began calling still others. The result was an arrangement to meet at Mrs. Hansen's on Sunday afternoon to talk the whole thing over. But by Sunday morning the number had grown to over fifty, so they asked Mrs. Henry Dreyfuss, the wife of the famous industrial designer, if they might use instead the larger Dreyfuss living room. Doris Dreyfuss cordially agreed.

By four o'clock Sunday afternoon some seventy men and women had pushed their way into the Dreyfuss house. Representatives of several social agencies were there, one of them colored. Three members of the Survey Committee itself were present—not in an official capacity but as individuals interested in a matter that concerned them. Mrs. Padelford was not among them. On hand too were some members of the Committee on Public Education—usually called COPE—an organization founded some months before to conduct impartial research work on Pasadena's schools.

The meeting was orderly and lacked any element of rabble rousing. Mrs. Hansen, an old hand at such things, was asked to take the chair. Many people had something to say. Some were there because, like Philip Fogg, they were strong admirers of Willard Goslin and liked what his administration had been doing. Others were incensed by the manner in which he had been asked to resign. Still others thought that the Board of Education should be persuaded to change its vote and wait for the report of the Survey Committee.

Philip Fogg and Lowell McAdam both talked with force and persuasion. Then a draft of a statement, to be published as a paid advertisement, was read, discussed, changed, and finally approved. Money was collected to pay for it. Mrs. Hansen and the Messrs. Fogg and McAdam were named to represent the committee in conversations with the Board and with Willard Goslin, to try to work out a settlement of differences.

Mrs. William Purcell, executive secretary of COPE, offered that organization's office and telephone as headquarters for the Action Committee. The meeting broke up about seven-thirty.

The next day—Monday—the committee's advertisement appeared. It read:

Attention!

BOARD OF EDUCATION

A Resolution Signed at a Mass Meeting of
Parents, Business and Professional Men
and Other Taxpayers:

In our opinion, the precipitate action of the Board of Education was taken as the result of undue pressure from a small and vocal group. Therefore we urge that the Board of Education not accept the resignation of Superintendent Willard E. Goslin until (1) there has been time for a complete clarification of the issues involved; (2) a full statement from the Board . . . has been given explaining its sudden action in Mr. Goslin's absence; (3) sufficient time has been allowed for an expression of the true sentiment of the community on the issues involved.

We further urge that (1) the Board of Education reaffirm its full support of the Survey Committee, and that (2) no change in the present system shall be made until such time as the results of the Survey are evaluated.

In a postscript, the committee asked that other citizens "with similar views" wire the Board and telephone the committee to register their names. Before the week was out, twelve hundred had done so, and the organization had a name: The Citizens Action Committee.

That same week end other organizations, new and old, were inspired to issue statements along the same lines. The Council of Parents and Teachers, which, as its statement said, is "specifically prohibited by policies and by-laws from taking a stand on controversial issues involving personalities," nevertheless urged "each member, as an individual citizen to exercise not only his right but his responsibility to keep the Board of Education informed. . . ." Another group of citizens had, like the Fogg group, met and formed themselves into the Pasadena Committee for Democracy in Education, and issued a statement, much on the order of Fogg's, that ended up by recommending that "the decision to dismiss Superintendent Goslin be reconsidered pending completion of the School Survey. . . ." An irate mother wrote in to ask: "Last summer the Board . . . was for both the tax increase and Goslin. Why are they now for the tax increase and not for Goslin? . . . Why does the Board . . . fear extremes of opinion among the teachers? . . ."

So many neighborhood meetings, small and large, had been held over the week end that the press was unable to keep track of them all, much less print their names. Even the *Star-News* began to sing a new tune, in an oddly off-key sort of way. On the day the wire to Mr. Goslin was published, the *Star-News* had come out with an editorial speculating as to who the new superintendent would be (the paper guessed wrong) and said that "in his difficult task, the new superintendent must be, and will be given, every helpfulness." Now, a few days later, it took another line. This time it proposed a "package deal" of cooperation between the Board and Willard Goslin. It proposed that the Board hold off accepting his resignation, and that "Dr. Goslin—without dispute an eminently recognized educator—pledge himself to be a little easier to work with, more often."

Willard Goslin had flown in quietly very late Saturday night and had been met at the airport by his wife and by nobody else. Monday morning he went as usual to his office in the Administration Building and put in a call for Milton Wopschall, whom he had told in his wire he would like to see that day. Mr. Wopschall was not in his office, and several times during the day when the superintendent tried again, the Board president was still unavailable.

That afternoon Philip Fogg and Mrs. Hansen, representing the Citizens Action Committee, called on Mr. Goslin and talked with him for an hour. The conversation centered around their desire that he hold off his resignation. Mr. Goslin made himself perfectly clear: the Board of Education represented the citizens, and if it was their will that he go, he would go. That, he said, was the democratic thing to do. His visitors countered with the suggestion that, possibly, they could persuade the Board of Education to sit down with the superintendent and work out a mutually satisfactory program—in the meantime rescinding their request for his resignation. Mr. Goslin agreed to that proposal, but it was understood that he would take no part in the proceedings until some action had first been taken by the Board.

Mrs. Hansen and Mr. Fogg left with the feeling that they had accomplished something. Their next step was to sound out the Board, and to this end they arranged a meeting with Milton Wopschall and Vernon Brydolf for the following Thursday. Before that meeting took place, however, two acts of this Pasadena drama, which was now at last open to the public, were staged. One was serious and impressive; the other was farcical and unreal.

On Tuesday afternoon the Board of Education was scheduled to hold its weekly meeting in the conference room at 351 South

Hudson. As four-thirty approached, a large crowd began to gather in the room and in the halls. It was soon apparent that the room would not hold them all, and the meeting was hastily shifted to the auditorium of McKinley Junior High School, across the playground. Again the people streamed in. They packed the ground floor and then they packed the gallery. When every one of the seats had been filled, the overflow stood in the aisles and at the rear of the large room.

At last the man they had been waiting for walked briskly down the aisle, flanked by three members of his staff. Willard Goslin was dressed in a well pressed light gray suit, a dotted tie, gray socks, and tan shoes. As he walked toward the platform, the audience rose. Someone started to applaud. Others started to cheer. Then suddenly the McKinley Auditorium was filled with standing, clapping, cheering people. Clearly this was Willard Goslin's day, these were Willard Goslin's friends.

President Wopschall opened the proceedings by explaining that he knew why so many people were there: they were interested in what the Board had done about Mr. Goslin. Then he went on to say that "the Board does not wish to entertain debates pro and con. But we are always willing to listen to the voice of the people. If you want to direct questions to the Board, we will do our best to answer them." Then he let it be known that this was only a "hearing," and that "final action" would be announced later. At that point someone in the audience shouted, "Chicken."

For an hour and a half the people had their say, and, most obviously, most of them there that day wanted the Board to undo what it had just done. A teacher from one of the junior highs got up to say he had not been able to find any evidences of the dissatisfaction with the superintendent the Board had mentioned in its wire. Others rose to agree with him. But most of the discussion revolved around the accusations of "turmoil" in the system. When a man, who identified himself as a father of three, demanded that the Board "document" that turmoil, Mr. Wopschall replied: "As a member of the Board I have known what turmoil is, whether you people believe it or not. There *is* turmoil, not only in the school system but in the community." Mr. Wopschall did not elaborate. And when he was asked whether he thought the turmoil was "created by a majority of the people," he was evasive. He said: "We have come to the conclusion that a large group of citizens is not completely satisfied with our school system. I can't say how large that group is, but to have a successful school system you have to have all the people with you."

On and on it went. Dr. Harold Case, minister of the First Methodist Church (two months later he was appointed president of Boston University), read a statement signed by forty-two Pasadena pastors. It was essentially the same as the Citizens Action Committee statement, urging the Board to hold off until the survey was completed. Philip Fogg gave the audience some details of the Sunday afternoon meeting at the Dreyfusses, and told how, since then, members of his committee had made "hundreds" of random telephone calls without producing one person who voiced dissatisfaction with the school system, its Administration, or Willard Goslin personally. "Will you," said Philip Fogg, squarely facing the Board members gazing down at him from the platform, "be big enough to back down and rescind your action?"

At once there came cries of, "Answer, answer," from the restive audience. And Mr. Wopschall did answer. "This Board," he said, "is always willing as individuals to back up whatever action it takes. In the past I have changed my vote. I can't speak for the Board on this question. But we've listened to the pros and cons, too, Mr. Fogg. We have visited the churches, the schools, business houses, and nearly every place in the city, and we don't get the same reaction you did, Mr. Fogg."

John Petterson of the School Development Council was there. He spoke, too, and his theme was a familiar one. He wanted to know whether previous speakers that afternoon weren't simply a "dissident minority." The true voice of the people, he said, had been expressed last June 2, when the Administration was defeated in the tax election. Mr. Petterson was not applauded. The SDC's attorney, Robert Aarons, then got up to tell the Board how much he liked its action in asking Mr. Goslin to quit. He was laughed at and roundly booed. And when he said, "Granted, for the sake of argument, that Mr. Goslin is able, granted that he is honest," they booed and laughed again, and even Willard Goslin gave him his slow wide grin.

At last someone asked the question everyone wanted answered: "Why was Goslin asked to resign?" And Mr. Wopschall answered once more: "In the opinion of the majority of the Board, the school system has been undergoing a tremendous amount of upheaval and turmoil. We felt that a great part of that turmoil was centered around Mr. Goslin."

The meeting ended pretty much where it had started; nothing had been accomplished. The Board was, apparently, still determined to get Mr. Goslin out. Mr. Goslin was, apparently, still determined to leave, if that was the way they wanted it. There still remained the Thursday conference Milton Wopschall and Vernon Brydolf were to have with the three members of the Citizens Action Committee. But before that, the second act of the drama was presented before another packed house. This one was held in the Council Chambers of the Pasadena City Hall, and it was produced by the California Senate Education Committee.

A few days earlier, the chairman of the committee, an old-line Republican named Nelson Dilworth, had announced that his two-day investigation was to look into "reports about subversive interferences with school operations." Whether Senator Dilworth's production was taking place at this particular moment in the history of Pasadena's schools because someone had planned it that way, or whether the timing was purely coincidence, is something no one was prepared to say. And at the end of the two days, the gentlemen from Sacramento did not make clear what they had accomplished. But while the hearings were in progress no one could have any doubt about what was on their minds.

First to testify was Milton Wopschall himself, and although he conducted himself well it could not be said that the committee showed him every courtesy. He was questioned at length on teaching in the Pasadena schools, and he defended the system as it stood with emphasis and clarity; he could not, he said, find anything subversive in the structure of the system itself or in the way the students were being taught. He was followed to the stand by Vernan Brydolf, whose testimony agreed with Milton Wopschall's, with the added observation that he felt that harmony was impossible in Pasadena so long as Willard Goslin remainded. Lawrence Lamb was asked for his views of Willard Goslin and replied, to the surprise of some: "I'm very fond of Mr. Goslin as an individual. I have respect for his educational ability. But he is not the proper man for Pasadena from an administrative standpoint . . . although he is a wonderful educator." He was the last Board member to be called. Mrs. Rinehart was not asked to testify.

The young Hungarian, George Gerbner, was called and questioned closely and at length. For a while, early in 1948—before it began to champion pro-Communist causes—George Gerbner had helped edit a publication called the *Progressive Citizen,* which was supporting Wallace for President. The committee dwelt for a long time on this, and perhaps because he had seen investigating committees in action in Central Europe, before his father was shot by the Communists, he did not conduct himself well.

For a long time, too, the schools' personnel director, Blair Nixon, was kept on the stand. He talked about the membership and strength of the Pasadena Education Association—the teachers' representative organization—and then got sufficiently wound up to suggest that the senators should really take a good look at the Pasadena situation and discover for themselves that it was a small pressure group which was making all the trouble. When he was asked whether he didn't think that the P.E.A. was also a pressure group, Mr. Nixon replied that it represented a majority of teachers; he was not, he said, in favor of minority groups speaking for the majority. The senators seemed quite friendly to Mr. Nixon until he made the mistake of using the term "witch hunt" in referring to the hearings.

Dr. Ernest Brower, by now something of an authority on education in Pasadena, was called and treated with consideration by the committee. His refrain was as usual: he saw the schools headed toward Socialism, he objected to teaching of sex, he felt that patriotism was being destroyed, he deplored the "smear" tactics of Goslin supporters (including packed meetings and "slanted" questions in Board of Education meetings), and he looked with some horror on visiting lecturers, summer workshops, and the like. At one point he said he agreed "100 per cent" with what Allen Zoll had written. But Dr. Brower's closing observation was particularly worth noting. Asked if his School Development Council had ever investigated Mr. Goslin, he replied that it had, and had found that the superintendent was a member of, among other things, the Bureau of Intercultural Education, UNESCO, and the National Conference of Christians and Jews. "Are these Communist groups?" a senator wanted to know. And Dr. Brower replied, "Well, they haven't been declared so."

Other School Development Councilors were called. Frances Bartlett was permitted to read a long statement entitled "A Memorandum on the Bureau of Intercultural Education." In the memorandum Mrs. Bartlett had compiled a partial list of members of the Bureau, which, she intimated, was subversive because the controversial William Heard Kilpatrick was on its board. Mrs. Bartlett's list included Harry Emerson Fosdick, the retired minister of Manhattan's Riverside Church (laughter from the audience), President Spyros Skouras of 20th Century Fox, Mrs. Kermit Roosevelt of the very Republican Oyster Bay (anti-New Deal) clan, and Mrs. Eleanor Roosevelt herself. Later, when pressed by reporters for her sources of the memorandum, Mrs. Bartlett referred them to Senator Dilworth, and he in turn told reporters it had been prepared by "two reputable private investigating firms in the East," but would comment no further.

Mrs. Bartlett also attempted to refute Lawrence Lamb's statement that he had found nothing subversive in the Pasadena schools. She told the committee that Mr. Lamb had discussed with her, at some length, the deplorable fact that a representative of the American Civil Liberties Union had spoken before a school meeting—seemingly the same one Dr. Brower had taken exception to in his letter to the school Board—and, too, had deplored, with her, the bringing of Dr. Kilpatrick to Pasadena. She also told the committee that Mr. Lamb had once said to her that Willard Goslin would "hang himself" if given enough time. (Mr. Lamb later denied to reporters that he had said any such thing.)

Willard Goslin was not subpoenaed by the committee. But he attended its sessions and was asked to testify. This he did readily. His theme, also, was familiar. Without bitterness or rancor he talked about the Pasadena system of public-school education. It was, he said, "on the threshold of one of the healthiest periods in the history of its education system." Coming from a man who had just been asked to quit his job as the head of that system, this statement received a rousing cheer from the crowded chamber. Senator Dilworth was obliged to rap his gavel several times before the uproar subsided. "My honest belief," Mr. Goslin went on, "is that although we have controversies and difficulties in the community now, in the final analysis we are going through the procedure typical in American history for communities to follow in determining what they want."

The superintendent was on the stand before the committee adjourned for lunch, and he climbed back on in the afternoon. He was questioned at length—on the summer workshops (he defended them, and denied they were tools whereby he could "indoctrinate" teachers with his personal theories of education); on the Zoll pamphlets (they were, he said, "an outright detriment to education"); on competitive grading of children (he said he believed in in competition, but, "I believe there are better ways to help the child grow and develop"); on the competitive enterprise system in business ("I am for it—without reservation"), and on down the list. By the time Willard Goslin was through, he had given many of his audience a strong impression that, right or wrong in what he had done in Pasadena, here was a man of integrity, principle, and purpose. If the Senate Committee came to the conclusion he was subversive, it did not say so, nor has anyone ever suggested as much since.

While the Senate hearings were still making headlines in Pasadena papers, those interested in keeping Willard Goslin in town were busy doing what they could without making headlines. As scheduled, the three representatives of the Citizens Action Committee, Philip Fogg, Lowell McAdam, and Betty Hansen, met with Milton Wopschall and Vernon Brydolf Thursday at the Pasadena Athletic Club. The atmosphere was friendly, but the committee members said what they had come there to say. In their opinion, and in the opinion of many other people they had talked to, the Board had made a great mistake in what it had done. Not only was the Board losing face in the community, Philip Fogg said, but the school system was suffering too. Then Mr. Wopschall and Mr. Brydolf were asked what, exactly, was wrong with Mr. Goslin. They both explained that it wasn't what their superintendent had done; it was the way he had gone about it. The old complaint was repeated about his not consulting them when they thought he should have. First, Milton Wopschall made this plain. Then Vernon Brydolf made it plain. Several times each of them said, with emphasis, that he had nothing against Willard Goslin's educational theories or practices.

As the talk went on, the three committee members became convinced they were on the right track. They admitted that Willard Goslin had not handled his public relations right. For the sake of argument they were ready to grant that perhaps he hadn't always sufficiently taken the Board into his confidence. Their suggestion seemed to make sense—why not see if the Board and their superintendent could not sit down, talk over their problems, and come up with an agreement that would satisfy everyone?

What then happened will, in the story of the Pasadena school crisis, be debated, perhaps, for a long time to come. Mrs. William Hansen, Philip Fogg, and Lowell McAdam left the Athletic Club that afternoon with one statement firm in their memories: Milton Wopschall said to them that, if Willard Goslin was agreed (and he already was agreed), "We pledge ourselves to rescind our request for his resignation, and to try to work out a program together." And toward this end they further promised that they would talk to Harriet Sterling and Lawrence Lamb, to try to bring about a unanimous rescind-vote. As the committee departed, the group decided upon a meeting —a meeting of all five school Board members and the three committee members—at ten o'clock Monday, once more at the Pasadena Athletic Club.

On Friday, while rumors were abroad that there existed the possibility of agreement, Mr. Goslin spoke at a rally of Pasadena schoolteachers. He was at his best. He talked about his two and a half years in Pasadena, and what he thought had been accomplished in that time. He spoke frankly and fully about the events of the past few weeks. He talked about the telegram sent to him in New York, and why he insisted that it be made public—"I felt a primary point involved was the teachers." He told how he had unsuccessfully tried to reach Board members on the Monday after his return. He stated that he had had a talk, only yesterday, with "representatives of the Board" to discuss how much he was to be paid in settlement. He assured the teachers that "my resignation was available from the moment it was asked for." He talked about the teachers themselves, and how much he was disturbed that "a great body like you can, in effect, be slyly indicted as an organization by irresponsible charges."

The next day the *Star-News,* in a well written report, said: "Many of those who did not join in the rising demonstration and applause when Mr. Goslin took the platform, arose and helped give him an ovation as he closed. He spoke as if he were talking to each member of the audience individually, straight-forward, quietly, without undue emotion. . . . Gloom was heavy in the hall as the audience moved quietly out. . . . Many had felt that Mr. Goslin might announce that he had harkened to the pressure of his friends and had changed his mind about resigning. His statement had dashed their hopes. The atmosphere was like that at a funeral."

That same Friday, just before setting off for the Army-Stanford football game in northern California, Milton Wopschall received a wire which may have given him pause. It was from Herbert C. Clish, Superintendent of San Francisco's public schools. Speaking for the Administrative Policies Commission of the California Association of School Administrators, of which he was chairman, Mr. Clish stated that the Commission "deplored" the "tactics" used in "demanding [Goslin's] resignation when he was several thousand miles away." The wire also suggested that the Board reconsider, and reminded it that Mr. Goslin was "one of the very competent administrators in the United States."

Over the week end Milton Wopschall sought out Mr. Clish

in San Francisco, and they discussed the Goslin matter for an hour. Although Mr. Clish had no responsibility toward or jurisdiction over public-school affairs in Pasadena, he was glad to give Mr. Wopschall his own point of view, based on long years of experience. Mr. Wopschall, when asked later whether he had indicated to Mr. Clish that he would change his vote, replied that he could not remember exactly what he had said, although he thought that he might have given the impression that he *could* change his mind. Still, he insisted he had made no promises. However, early on the following Monday morning Mrs. Rinehart, the Goslin faithful on the Board, talked to Mr. Clish on the long-distance telephone. He told her, in effect, that he thought "you now have two members of the Board with you."

Whatever else happened over that week end no one now will say. But one thing was certain. On Monday morning, the school Board met with the Action Committee. This was the meeting on which Mr. Fogg and his friends had placed so much hope and faith. But it produced results diametrically opposed to those the committee thought it would. All the old anti-Goslin refrains were again repeated. No longer was any of the four simply objecting to the way Willard Goslin had gone about his job. They had revived the cry that the school tax election could never be passed next June if he were still in office. They stressed the fact that there would be no newspaper support if Goslin stayed. They spoke again of "turmoil" in the city, and of how unhappy some of the teachers were. Plainly, they indicated that Willard Goslin must go, with firm Mrs. Rinehart firmly disagreeing. The previous Thursday's meeting and the talk with Mr. Clish notwithstanding, Mr. Wopschall was adamant. And although it was evident that he and Mr.

Brydolf were irritated because they thought Mr. Goslin had slighted the Board in his Friday speech to the teachers, the Action Committee was surprised and dismayed that, contrary to its confident expectation, a complete reversal had come about.

Of all those at the meeting Lawrence Lamb was the most outspoken. He announced that he thought "this is one of the most Communistic things that has ever been done in this community. My lawyer told me not to come here, and not to talk. But I have to say something." No one knew quite what Mr. Lamb meant, but, before they could find out, Vernon Brydolf broke in to give his fellow member a good lacing. This byplay did no good, however, and had no effect on the tenor or the outcome of the meeting. It was now plain, as of eleven o'clock Monday morning, November 20, that for whatever reasons, the Board of Education of the City of Pasadena was still, or once more, bent on getting rid of Willard Goslin.

There was nothing more to be done. Philip Fogg had had several long private talks with Mr. Goslin through the past week, and the superintendent had, time and again, restated his position: if the Board wanted him to resign, he would do so. And, as Mr. Goslin had said, he had had two discussions with the Messrs. Brydolf and Wopschall concerning the one thing still to be decided—how much he should be paid for the eighteen months his contract would still be in effect. By now that had been agreed upon: Pasadena's schools would give him $23,250 as payment in full for services that might have been rendered. All that remained was for this settlement to be made legal at a Board meeting and for the Board to accept his resignation.

Both of these things happened the next afternoon in the

third and last act of the drama. Long before it was time for the Board to meet, the parking lots flanking the Administration Building were jammed with cars. Again an enormous crowd surged through the halls, up the stairs, and into the conference room itself. But this time, through oversight or by design, the meeting was not shifted to the auditorium.

The first member of the Board to walk in through the side door was Mrs. Gladys Rinehart. By this time she, like all the other members of the cast, was familiar to the crowd. They gave her a rousing welcome. Then in came the others, one by one. They were greeted with silence. Finally Willard Goslin entered, and a shout went up from the audience.

After the meeting was formally opened, Mr. Goslin walked over to the center of the dais and handed Milton Wopschall a piece of paper. Mr. Wopschall then haltingly read aloud Willard Goslin's resignation as superintendent of Pasadena's Public Schools. It was to be effective at the close of business the following night. The statement was brief and to the point. At its end Mr. Goslin had written: "This school system and community are filled with fine and able people. It has been a privilege to work with them. I want to thank the members of the Board of Education and all others who believe in good schools for the numerous courtesies which have been extended to me."

Vernon Brydolf thereupon read a resolution recommending the acceptance of the resignation, and the terms thereof. It was duly approved. And then Milton Wopschall announced that Willard Goslin would like to say a few words. The silence in the room was intense as Mr. Goslin leaned forward and began to deliver his valedictory to the Board he had worked with since July of 1948.

First, said Mr. Goslin, he wanted to tell why he had not

resigned at once, and privately. He listed five reasons. For one thing, he wanted to make it clear that he felt teachers had "the right and privilege to stand up *for* or *against* any question" and hence he felt it was necessary for him to register his objection to the Board's statement that the teachers were acting as a pressure group. Second, he felt that because a superintendent of public schools was "the educational leader of the community" the telegram should be made public. Third, he felt that "the action of the Board . . . was a threat to [the] status" of the many men and women who are superintendents of schools. Fourth, he pointed out that the telegram had made "no mention . . . of the basis of [financial] settlement." And fifth, he "was unable to step out . . . quietly . . . when a major school survey was in prospect. . . . The implications of such a step were unacceptable to me."

Having thus explained himself, Mr. Goslin next said he wished to make this position clear. "In America," he said, "we are dedicated to representative government. This nation to my mind has had its best experience with representative government in terms of laymen elected to boards of education to manage the affairs of the public schools. I am so committed to this way of developing and managing education that I am unable to be in contempt of the elected representatives of the community when they have asked me to resign."

Then Mr. Goslin had his say on how he felt about education as it stands in the United States. "We are," he said, "in an exceedingly difficult position. . . . Each of us feels that our freedom is in jeopardy. We are threatened from without. I think we are threatened even more from within. I know of no better way to wreck everything that we think is good in America than to begin to destroy ourselves, one by one, institution by institution, community by community, throughout the land. To keep this from happening here won't you give away some of your animosities and differences and try to find common ground to stand on in support of public education? . . . It is only through your common interest and joined efforts that you can underwrite your own school system and help your neighbors to underwrite their school systems. . . ."

And with that, Mr. Goslin bowed out. "I shall take away no ill feelings," he said, "when I leave Pasadena—rather, a deep regret that I was unable to lead this community to a level which would have produced the best school system in America."

The Board meeting was now over, and Willard Goslin was no longer to be superintendent of Pasadena's schools. As the people slowly left the conference room that November afternoon, some of them were crying.

17

Aftermath

On December 4 a friendly, gray-haired, neatly dressed man with gleaming bifocals sat down at the desk Willard Goslin had so recently vacated. His name was Frank Ralph Walkup. He was the new acting superintendent of Pasadena's public schools.

"Educationally," Mr. Walkup announced after his appointment, "I am considered a middle-of-the-roader. I believe in retaining the best of the old and adding the best of the new in a school instruction program." There was every likelihood that Mr. Walkup knew what he was talking about. For the last twenty-two of his fifty-six years he had been in the Pasadena school system, and since 1939 he had been principal of McKinley Junior High School. His work had been sound, safe, and sane. He had never said anything or done anything to indicate that his educational philosophy was alarming to those who disapproved of Modern Education. And hence it was not surprising that as soon as Frank Walkup was installed in office the School Development Council came out for him officially and without reservation. Dr. Ernest Brower announced he was personally pleased. So did Cay Hallberg and Frances Bartlett and a great many others who could not contain their pleasure when Willard Goslin resigned. Louise Padelford, who was so satisfied with Mr. Goslin's leaving that she resigned from the Survey Committee while she was still in New York, was even more satisfied when Mr. Walkup went in.

Frank Wells, although at the time as enthusiastic as his friends, was soon too embroiled in certain affairs of his own to pay much public attention to school-system activities. In February of 1951, a civil suit was filed against him for fraud and embezzlement. Later, when he declined to produce the books of his trench-digging-equipment company, as ordered by the examining judge, he was held in contempt, a matter which, at present writing, is hanging fire in the Pasadena courts.

Unlike Mr. Wells, Mrs. Hallberg, Dr. Brower, and their friends, a number of other people in Pasadena, inside the system and out, did not approve of some of the things Mr. Walkup and the Board immediately set out to do. On November 14, when the request for Willard Goslin's resignation was bringing in to the Board a steady stream of protesting telegrams, Milton Wopschall issued a statement to the press which seemed plain despite its lapse in grammar: "The Board of Education wishes to reaffirm their full support of the School Survey Committee and further state that the Board will make no change in educational policies or additional changes in personnel until such time as the results of the survey are evaluated." That was clear enough, and a few weeks later Mr. Wopschall and his Board, at a meeting with the Survey Committee, again promised no changes—although this time the significant word "major" was inserted in front of "change." In view of the fact that the Board had not given the Survey Committee even the slightest hint that it was planning to ask for Mr. Goslin's resignation, much less consult it, these reassurances were encouraging.

But now Frank Walkup was taking to his job with every evidence of enthusiasm and pleasure. He hadn't been in office very long before he handed down the word that the *Clearing House* was to be discontinued. This was not interesting news to anyone outside the system; but within the system the publication had significance as a means of disseminating information to teachers, and, further, as a means for their sending back complaints and criticisms to the Central Office, the *Clearing House* in its short life was considered valuable. Mr. Walkup, however, thought it a waste of time, paper, and money; and the money, he said, "could better be spent on the pupils," although when he was asked how much the paper was costing, he said he had not tried to find out. Next he quietly passed out word that there would be no workshop next summer. "I have no objection to summer workshops," he told a reporter. "They are a good part of in-service training. Many fine ones have been held. But I don't think we are ready for one in Pasadena." Then, with the due consent of the Board, Blair Nixon was removed as personnel director and made principal of a new elementary school. And the very man Willard Goslin had moved out was brought back into the personnel office. It was this that caused one member of the staff, preparing his own resignation, to remark that the motto of the new Administration seemed to be, "Move slowly, except backward."

When it came to young Gerbner, the Hungarian-born former paratrooper who was still a probationary teacher, the new Administration executed some intricate footwork. Early in February he was told that his contract would not be renewed the following year. This news came as a complete surprise to his superiors in the school where he was teaching; they had not been consulted, and they strongly urged that he be retained. And in the end he was retained, possibly because by this time the School Development Council was beginning to take credit for the swift post-Goslin changes in the system. It must, therefore, have been something of a shock to the School Development Council when Mr. Gerbner was informed that his contract would be renewed after all.

Not all the comings and goings were Administration inspired: three members of Willard Goslin's immediate staff—Karol Greeson and two secretaries, Mary Bates and Helen Flittner, both of whom Mr. Goslin had hired from within the system—quit when their boss did. Mrs. Jane Hood, the able curriculum coordinator whom Mr. Goslin had borrowed from the University of Southern California, decided that the new Administration did not hold out the rich promise she envisioned for Pasadena education under Willard Goslin, and she went back to the university. Several other members of the staff went quietly out hunting for jobs where they thought the atmosphere would be more to their liking.

By the time these people had gone, and Blair Nixon had been shifted, rumors started going the rounds that the Board was considering making Mr. Walkup's appointment permanent. This was too much for the Survey Committee. As the Board well knew, it had empowered the Survey Committee, even before Willard Goslin had been asked to resign, to hire two well known experts, Dr. Clyde Hill of Yale's Department of Education and Dr. Lloyd Morrisett of the University of California at Los Angeles, to conduct the details of the investigation. They were already hard at work. As the Board also knew, the survey was to cost the system some $50,000. And now here were a number of Board-backed Administration moves which were making the work of the Survey so difficult that its usefulness was seriously impaired.

Consequently, on February 6 the Survey Committee's chairman, James Boyle, addressed a letter to the Board. "The time is now here," he wrote, "when the actual work of the Pasadena School Survey is under way. It seems appropriate, therefore, that our Committee express to you at this time the hope that during the coming critical months the stability of the school system be maintained to the highest possible degree. A survey of a rapidly changing situation can clearly have but little meaning."

To bring about stability, Mr. Boyle made three recommendations—first, that "in line with the commitment already made to us by the Board," it should make "no important changes in the personnel" while the survey was going on, and if any were in prospect, the committee "would like to be consulted"; second, that Mr. Walkup remain acting superintendent, but only acting superintendent, until the survey was finished; and third, that if there was to be a tax election for the elementary-school district next June, any new levy should be for one year only, so that longer term levies could be judged in light of what the survey had uncovered.

Mr. Boyle's letter was duly read in Board meeting. Its contents irritated some of the members. But the committee would not back down: it had been given a job to do, and it had hired capable men to execute the assignment, and, as one of its members observed privately, "We are trying to take a picture, but we can't take it when nobody will stand still."

If Mr. Walkup was disturbed by these developments, he did not show it. He had made it clear from the beginning that he wanted no part of what had happened during the last few hectic months. All that to him was "water under the bridge." And he was now making it equally clear that if he was not out actually to please as many of the old-line dissident groups as he could, certainly he was not planning to do anything to displease them, even if a forward-looking and constructive program of education might suffer in the process.

By the end of February, 1951, the future of Pasadena's schools was cloudy and uncertain. What would happen at the Board election in June was anyone's guess. Two places are to be filled—Harriet Sterling's and Milton Wopschall's, either by them or by two others. Miss Sterling's plans were indefinite because in February she had the great misfortune of breaking her leg while on a trip to Mexico. Mr. Wopschall has said he would not run again, but he has been known to change his mind before. Late in February, the Citizens Action Committee, which had worked so hard to keep Mr. Goslin in office, and the research-minded Committee on Public Education (COPE) joined forces to form a new organization, retaining the name of COPE. Its immediate purpose was to work out and vigorously support a slate of Board candidates who would show the most promise of promoting sound education.

COPE's membership and many other people hoped that what had just happened would never happen again in Pasadena. Whether it does or not will depend on the people of Pasadena, just as the destinies of every other American community depend on the vigilance of its electorate.

18

"If We Are to Retain Freedom and Democracy—"

Willard Goslin left Pasadena on February 16, 1951. Two weeks later he and his wife and their daughter Jane boarded a freighter in New Orleans for a leisurely voyage to the Far and Middle East. After that would come a European summer working partly with underprivileged students in Western Europe and partly with adult educational and religious groups. In September he would go to George Peabody College in Nashville to head a Division on School Administration and Community Development.

Thoughtful citizens in Pasadena did not feel sorry for Willard Goslin because he had been asked to resign. They knew he did not want or need their sympathy. What bothered them—and bothered them badly—was the stark fact that their city's schools had emerged from the activities of the past year much the worse for wear; and unless they did something about it, as thinking individuals and as well organized representatives of the better elements in the community, their public schools might be a long time recovering, a long time regaining their reputable place at education's council tables. And the citizens of Pasadena now knew what citizens of many other communities still might not know: that what had happened in Pasadena could easily happen in other cities where modern educational systems were under attack.

In the December issue of his promotional organ *Educational Guardian,* Allen A. Zoll did some crowing about Willard Goslin's resignation. "Another Victory," he labeled it; and although he described as "not accurate" some published reports to the effect that his National Council for American Education had been responsible for getting Mr. Goslin out, he did claim that "the Council itself and a number of our members did have a large part in it." Then, in his January issue, Allen Zoll took a look back, and another look ahead, at other educational fronts.

"As well as can be estimated," Mr. Zoll wrote, "there has been about ten times as much public attention paid this past year to the situation in the schools as there was in previous years. While NCAE cannot take credit for all this, it can take much of the credit . . . the spearhead in the fight . . . the outstanding leader in arousing the people. The millions of pieces of literature we have sent out during the past two and a half years, to tens of thousands of molders of public opinion—editors, commentators, columnists, heads of clubs, state legislators, school officials, boards of education, etc. have had an effect—an important effect." And, continued Mr. Zoll with comparable modesty, "hundreds of local school improvement groups" had been "aided, stimulated to action or formed" by his NCAE.

How much Allen Zoll was overstating the case no one can say. It would be greatly to his benefit for everyone to take him too seriously, to believe that his power is as great as he claims. It would be just as erroneous, however, to disregard Allen Zoll completely. For this much is certain: The Zoll pattern is the same as the Pasadena pattern, the Zoll attack on education is the same as the Pasadena attack on education. First it admits the importance of public education; then it proceeds to damn every phase of a modern public-school system: it is leading the nation toward Socialism, its textbooks are written by Communists, it pays too little attention to fundamental educational principles, it fails to adhere to facts, it fails to avoid controversial issues, and so on. And the strategy Mr. Zoll applauds so vigorously is the strategy that was followed in Pasadena—the formation of a self-appointed school committee, without real community backing, more destructive than constructive in its approach; a flood of material to the press denouncing the system as it stands; the welcome into its fold of all dissatisfied parents, of superpatriots and of ambitious, frustrated individuals; mass meetings and public forums where only their views, and not opposing views, are aired; the repetition over and over again of hearsay, half-truths, and educational clichés.

In these uneasy days, honest, well meaning citizens are often vulnerable to the campaigns of all sorts of infiltrating minority pressure groups. Unless these citizens learn to recognize such dangers and awaken to what free public-school education should mean to them and to their children, many of them will swallow all too willingly—hook, line, and sinker—the kind of bait sold by propagandists like Zoll. It can only be hoped that the citizens of such cities as Denver and Minneapolis, San Diego and Upper Arlington, Ohio, where attacks on education have been reaching alarming proportions, will take heed of something Willard Goslin wrote for the magazine *Educational Leadership* in March, 1949, when he was still Superintendent of Schools in Pasadena.

"Freedom and democracy," he wrote, "*as we know them* exist only on this continent at the present time. If we are to retain freedom and democracy and make it possible for other peoples to benefit from them, the American people must prove to believe deeply enough in the dignity of the individual and in the basic American ideals of free speech, freedom of religion, free press, and public education to meet successfully the conflict of ideologies which is now taking place in the world."

Publishers' Note

Up-to-date and unbiased information concerning public education in America is available to everyone for the asking. The United States Office of Education in Washington is, of course, a source of pertinent data. The National Education Association, with headquarters at 1201 16th St., N.W., Washington 6, D.C., is another. Its current membership comprises over 450,000 teachers, superintendents, and principals on elementary, secondary, and college levels and involves more than 3,500 affiliated local associations. The American Association of School Administrators, of which Willard Goslin was president during his first year in Pasadena, is a very important division of the N.E.A.

Two years ago a group of leading laymen headed by Roy E. Larsen, president of Time Inc. and onetime Overseer of Harvard University, founded the National Citizens Commission for the Public Schools with the purpose of encouraging a broader, more effective, and constructive interest of citizens in the aims and opportunities of public education. To date the Commission has concentrated on helping in the formation of representative community groups for the purpose of improving local public schools. It acts as a clearinghouse to enable existing groups to benefit from the experience of others, in the hope that community efforts now being carried on in isolation can benefit from the continuing encouragement and pooling of information which the Commission provides. It also conducts workshops where school administrators, teachers, and school board members can meet and discuss ways and means of promoting better education. It helps develop articles in newspapers and national magazines and has been cooperating actively with the Advertising Council's "Better Schools" Campaign, which reaches millions of Americans each month through radio, car cards, newspapers, billboards, and magazines. All of these activities contribute toward the disinterested end of creating a greater public understanding and appreciation of public education. The Commission's headquarters are located at 2 West 45th Street, New York 19.

Other organizations equipped to provide relevant facts and figures are: National School Boards Association, 450 East Ohio St., Chicago 11, Ill.; Rural Editorial Service, University of Chicago, 5835 Kimbark Ave., Chicago 37, Ill.; and National Congress of Parents and Teachers, the publishers of the official Parent-Teacher Association magazine, *National Parent-Teacher,* 600 S. Michigan Boulevard, Chicago 5, Ill.